KU-513-372

Copyright© 2000 by Que® Corporation

International Standard Book Number: 0-7897-2270-4

Library of Congress Catalog Card Number: 99-65926

Printed in the United States of America

First Printing: December 1999

02   01   00   99   4   3   2   1

Trademarks

Warning and Disclaimer

Executive Editor
Greg Wiegand

Acquisitions Editor
Angelina Ward

Development Editor
Gregory Harris

Managing Editor
Thomas F. Hayes

Project Editor
Leah Kirkpatrick

Copy Editor
Kay Hoskin

Indexer
Heather McNeill

Technical Editor
John Purdum

Proofreader
Jeanne Clark

Production
Cyndi Davis-Hubler

How to Use This Book

It's as Easy as 1-2-3

Each part of this book is made up of a series of short, instructional lessons, designed to help you understand basic information that you need to get the most out of your computer hardware and software.

Click: Click the left mouse button once.

Double-click: Click the left mouse button twice in rapid succession.

Right-click: Click the right mouse button once.

Pointer Arrow: Highlights an item on the screen you need to point to or focus on in the step or task.

Selection: Highlights the area onscreen discussed in the step or task.

Click & Type: Click once where indicated and begin typing to enter your text or data.

 Tips and Warnings give you a heads-up for any extra information you may need while working through the task.

2 Each task includes a series of quick, easy steps designed to guide you through the procedure.

How to Drag: Point to the starting place or object. Hold down the mouse button (right or left per instructions), move the mouse to the new location, then release the button.

Drag

Drop

1 Each step is fully illustrated to show you how it looks onscreen.

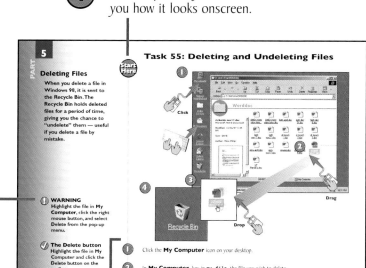

Task 55: Deleting and Undeleting Files

Deleting Files

When you delete a file in Windows 98, it is sent to the Recycle Bin. The Recycle Bin holds deleted files for a period of time, giving you the chance to "undelete" them — useful if you delete a file by mistake.

WARNING
Highlight the file in **My Computer**, click the right mouse button, and select **Delete** from the pop-up menu.

The Delete button
Highlight the file in **My Computer** and click the **Delete** button on the toolbar.

1 Click the **My Computer** icon on your desktop.

2 In **My Computer**, key in **my file** the file you wish to delete.

3 Press and hold down the left mouse button and **drag** the icon into the **Recycle Bin**.

4 Release the mouse button to drop the file into the **Recycle Bin**.

3 Items that you select or click in menus, dialog boxes, tabs, and windows are shown in **bold**. Information you type is in a **special font**.

Next Step: If you see this symbol, it means the task you're working on continues on the next page.

End Task: Task is complete.

Introduction to Web Page Publishing

It wasn't that long ago that the perception of a Webmaster was close to that of a god. Those also were the days when you had to know how to hand-code HTML to create Web pages. That meant launching a text editor of some kind and scribbling all kinds of arcane formatting codes. Thank goodness those days are over! Now anyone can develop a Web page—thanks to WYSIWYG (what you see is what you get) programs such as FrontPage Express and Netscape Composer. If you can use word-processing tools, such as Microsoft Word, you can create Web pages because much of the functionality is the same. Creating Web pages today is a breeze.

The tools you need to begin developing your own Web pages are your PC, Windows (Windows 95, 98, or NT), an Internet account, and your own creativity. The only other tool you need is the one you are reading right now.

In this book, you'll find not only clear, simple steps for creating Web pages and making them look great, but also instructions for getting a free Web page authoring tool. The tool and the steps work together to make you an aspiring Webmaster—the *Easy* way.

PART I

Getting a Web Page Authoring Tool

Before we jump right in and start having fun, we must first check to see if you have a Web authoring tool. A Web authoring tool allows you to create a Web page in much the same way you create a document with a word processor. The better Web authoring tools, like the better word processors, are called **WYSIWYG** (what you see is what you get), because while you're working on a Web page, the tool shows you what the page will look like online.

Many popular WYSIWYG Web authoring tools are available. This book uses one of those tools, Microsoft's FrontPage Express, for three reasons: It's free, it's easy to get, and it's an excellent tool to begin learning about Web authoring. In this part of the book, you learn how to get FrontPage Express (or find out whether you already have it!), and get started using it.

Note that FrontPage Express has much in common with other WYSIWYG Web authoring tools, including its bigger brother, FrontPage. (FrontPage is Microsoft's pro-level Web tool, not to be confused with FrontPage Express.) The experience you gain here in FrontPage Express will move right along with you, if and when you choose to move up to another tool. If you have another simple Web editor, such as Netscape Composer, you'll find most of the steps to be fairly similar.

Tasks

There's a good chance you already have FrontPage Express and can skip Tasks 2, 3, and 4. FrontPage Express is a part of Microsoft Internet Explorer 4 and 5, is included free on many PCs, and is piggy-backed free in many other tools (especially Microsoft software) and products, such as Windows 98. So you may already have FrontPage Express. But, here's how to find out for sure.

✓ Installing Internet Explorer 5

On some computers (especially new ones), Internet Explorer 5 has not yet been installed. However, an icon for installing it should appear on the desktop. This icon, sometimes labeled Set Up Internet Explorer, starts the installation process. If you don't have FrontPage Express, but do see the Internet Explorer icon on your desktop, skip ahead to Task 4.

Task 1: Do You Already *Have* a Web-Authoring Tool?

(1) From your Windows taskbar, click the **Start** button.

(2) Depending on the location chosen during installation, choose **Programs**, and then click **Internet Tools** or **Internet Explorer**.

(3) If FrontPage Express appears in the Internet Tools or Internet Explorer menu, you can skip ahead to Task 5. If not, see Task 2.

Task 2: Surfing to Microsoft's Web Site to Get an Authoring Tool

Click

If you don't already have FrontPage Express, you can get it (free, of course) simply by installing Internet Explorer 5 and selecting the right options. It's also included with many Microsoft tools. The following task shows you how to get it from the Internet.

✅ Getting IE5 on CD-ROM

On the Internet Explorer Web site, you'll find not only a link for getting Internet Explorer online, but also a link for ordering Internet Explorer on CD for a small fee ($6.95 + tax, at this writing). Internet Explorer is a very large program, so it may take an hour or more to download from the Internet, depending on your modem speed. If you don't like tying up your phone line, you can order it on CD. In addition, you might want to check out the **System Requirements** link from the site menu on the left of the page to review what you need to download and run Internet Explorer.

1 Open your Web browser (a previous version of Internet Explorer, Netscape Navigator, or whatever you usually use to surf the Web) and connect to the Internet.

2 Go to Microsoft's Internet Explorer Web site at **www.microsoft.com/ie/default .htm**.

Task 3: Downloading the Setup Program

Getting Internet Explorer
and FrontPage Express
from the Web happens in
two parts. The first is
getting the setup program
ie5setup.exe, as described
here. The second is using
that program to complete
the download and setup, as
described in Task 4.

 Click

 Click

Click

✓ **Be Prepared for a Delay**

The Saving dialog box
displays a time estimate
to let you know
approximately how long it
will take to download the
setup file. So, now would
be a good time to catch up
on that reading (like this
book!), take a nap, or do
whatever your heart
desires.

① Go to Microsoft's Internet Explorer Web site (**www.microsoft.com/ie/default.htm**) as described in Task 2.

② Click the **Download Now** button.

③ Select **Save This Program to Disk** and then click **OK**.

Click

④
Choose a folder (or your desktop) to save the Internet Explorer setup program in, and click **Save** to begin downloading the ie5setup.exe file.

⑤
Upon completion, the Saving dialog box disappears if the **Close This Dialog Box When Download Completes** check box is checked.

✓ **Check for Updated Versions**

In the example shown here, the latest release of Internet Explorer 5 is "Internet Explorer 5." But new versions come out from time to time, and by the time you go to download, there may be an Internet Explorer version 5+. That version may include an upgraded version of FrontPage Express. You should download the latest version, whatever it is.

Task 4: Installing Internet Explorer and FrontPage Express

The Internet Explorer setup program sets up Internet Explorer (and FrontPage Express) on your PC. If you downloaded the setup program (as in Task 3), then the program automatically downloads the rest of Internet Explorer from the Web; if you have the setup program on CD, then it automatically copies the Internet Explorer files from the CD.

I recommend that you have all programs closed before installing Internet Explorer, because you will be required to restart your computer after the installation completes. Now on with the show.

✓ Your Browser Doesn't Matter

Again, you do not have to use Internet Explorer for surfing the Web in order to use FrontPage Express. You can continue to use whatever you usually use for Web surfing, and use FrontPage Express for Web authoring jobs.

Start Here

Double-Click

Click

Click

Click

Click

Click

Click

1 Connect to the Internet (or insert the CD, if you have Internet Explorer 5 on CD).

2 Locate the file folder to which you downloaded the setup program and double-click the **ie5setup.exe** file icon.

3 Select **I Accept the Agreement** and click **Next**.

4 Select the **Install Minimal, or Customize Your Browser** option and click **Next**.

Next Step

Click

Click

Click

Click

Click

Click

Installing Help

Installing Internet Explorer Help and Additional Web Fonts are optional. But, it doesn't hurt to have the Help to use as a reference. And you can always use more fonts.

Performing a Custom Installation

With previous versions of Internet Explorer, you would select a typical install to install both the browser and FrontPage Express. However, with Internet Explorer 5, FrontPage Express is only installed if you choose to install it. So, doing a custom install saves you the extra step of having to perform two installations—one for the browser and one for FrontPage Express.

Choosing Other Installation Options

The other options you can install are up to you. They are not required to perform the tasks in this book. However, you may want to play with them later. So, it's up to you.

5 Make sure you check the following selections: **Internet Explorer 5 Web Browser**, **Internet Explorer Help**…

6 …**FrontPage Express**, **Web Publishing Wizard**, and **Additional Web Fonts**. Click **Next**.

7 Click **Yes** to continue.

8 Accept the default download site by clicking **Next**. Click **Finish** to restart your computer.

Task 5: Opening FrontPage Express

Start Here

After Internet Explorer and FrontPage Express have been installed, you are ready to start creating Web pages. Here's how to open FrontPage Express and get ready to work.

Click

Click

Click

Click

Click

✓ **Opening a Blank Document**

When FrontPage Express opens, it automatically opens a new, blank Web page file. You can start typing right away to begin creating your first Web page—although in Part 2, "Building Your First Web Page," you'll discover even easier ways to get a new page going.

1. From your Windows taskbar, click the **Start** button.

2. Click **Programs**.

3. Click **Accessories** or, depending on the locations chosen during installation, **Internet Explorer**, and then click **Internet Tools**. Click **FrontPage Express**.

4. FrontPage Express opens.

End Task

Task 6: Discovering FrontPage Express's Toolbars

Start Here

Format Toolbar

Standard Toolbar

Forms Toolbar

2 Click

3

Click

4 Click

You perform many functions in FrontPage Express by clicking buttons on three toolbars: Standard, Format, and Forms. The toolbars appear as three rows of buttons near the top of the FrontPage Express window, and each can be displayed (for ready use) or hidden (to free up more screen area for examining your creations.)

✓ Getting Information from ToolTips

Every button (or list box) on the toolbars has a "ToolTip," a name that appears to identify the button. To learn the name of any button or list box, point to it (don't click) and pause a moment without moving the mouse.

✓ Scanning the ToolTip List

To quickly see the names of all the buttons in one toolbar, point to the button or list box that's farthest to the left, but don't click. Move your mouse to the right and as you pass each button, its name displays.

1 Open FrontPage Express and look at the three rows of buttons beneath the menu bar.

2 Click **View**. On the menu, a check mark appears next to the name of each toolbar that is currently displayed.

3 To hide a toolbar, click its name.

4 To re-display a toolbar you've hidden, click **View** and click the toolbar's name again.

End Task

Building Your First Web Page

So you're probably staring at a blank page thinking about how you should begin. That's where FrontPage Express can really help. When you create your first Web pages, it helps to have a head start—a basic prefab page or template you can mold to your own liking.

That's what FrontPage Express's Personal Home Page Wizard provides—a head start. It doesn't give you a finished page all by itself; you still need to go in and personalize the page that the wizard produces. But you'll find that creating your first page is easier when you don't start out with a blank page. The tasks in this part show you how to use the wizard to crank out that first page in a flash.

Of course, you may soon want to create a new, blank Web page you can fill with your own ideas from scratch. By the end of this chapter, you'll know how to do that, too.

Tasks

Task 1: Starting the Personal Home Page Wizard

We begin your trip through the Personal Home Page Wizard by starting a new page in FrontPage Express. So, here we go.

Click 2

Click 3

Click 4

1. Open FrontPage Express.

2. Click **File**, and then select **New**.

3. Click **Personal Home Page Wizard**.

4. Click **OK**.

Task 2: Choosing What to Include on the Page

The Personal Home Page Wizard provides several different options from which to choose. Each option is used to display different types of information on the Web page. You choose which sections you want on your Web page.

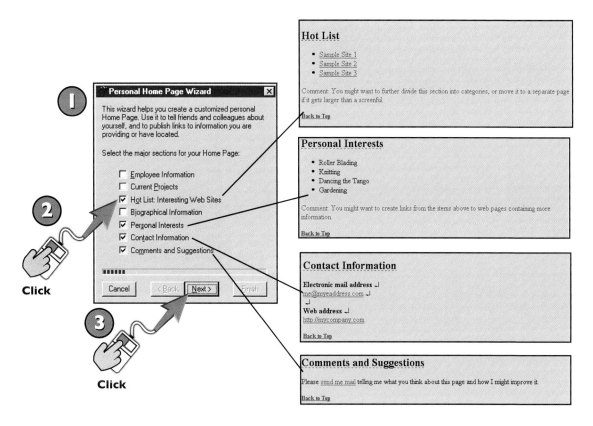

Hot List

- Sample Site 1
- Sample Site 2
- Sample Site 3

Comment: You might want to further divide this section into categories, or move it to a separate page if it gets larger than a screenful.

Back to Top

Personal Interests

- Roller Blading
- Knitting
- Dancing the Tango
- Gardening

Comment: You might want to create links from the items above to web pages containing more information.

Back to Top

Contact Information

Electronic mail address ↵
me@myeaddress.com ↵
↵
Web address ↵
http://mycompany.com

Back to Top

Comments and Suggestions

Please send me mail telling me what you think about this page and how I might improve it.

Back to Top

Personal Home Page Wizard

This wizard helps you create a customized personal Home Page. Use it to tell friends and colleagues about yourself, and to publish links to information you are providing or have located.

Select the major sections for your Home Page:

- ☐ Employee Information
- ☐ Current Projects
- ☑ Hot List: Interesting Web Sites
- ☐ Biographical Information
- ☑ Personal Interests
- ☑ Contact Information
- ☑ Comments and Suggestions

Cancel < Back Next > Finish

Click

Click

① Review the list of items, and decide what information you want to include on your Web page.

② For practice, leave check marks only next to **Hot List**, **Personal Interests**, **Contact Information**, and **Comments and Suggestions**.

③ Click **Next**.

✓ **Checking a Check Box**
To add a check mark to an empty check box, point to the box and click. To remove a check mark from a check box, point to the checked box and click.

Task 3: Naming the Page and Its File

To save and use your Web page, you must give it a filename. You should give your Web page files short, simple filenames, always ending in **.htm** or **.html**. Usually, the first Web page you create is considered the "home" page. So, a lot of people call their first Web page just that, home.html. The home page is the place from which all links originate. (You'll learn more about links in Part 4, "Making Links.") In addition to a filename, all Web pages also have a title, which identifies the page contents to visitors.

Click

✓ **Changing Previous Decisions in a Wizard**
At any point while working with the wizard, you can click **Back** to move backward to earlier tasks and change the choices you made. Your choices don't become final until you click **Finish**.

1 In the **Page URL** box, type a simple filename for your Web page file and end the name with **.htm** or **.html**.

2 In the **Page Title** box, type a descriptive title for your page.

3 Click **Next**.

Task 4: Choosing the Style for Your List of Links

Start Here

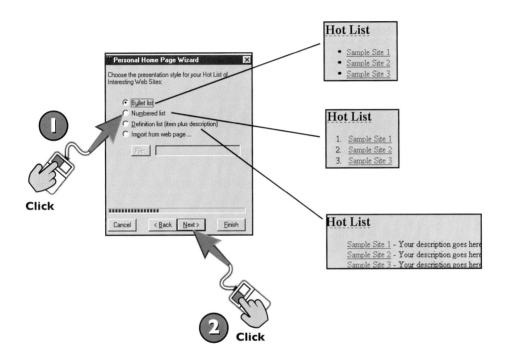

Click

①

②

Click

The wizard can whip up a snazzy list of links—a "Hot List"—so that your visitors can jump straight from your page to other pages you want to share with them. Actually, the links are "dummy" links—links that don't go anywhere—until you tell them where to go, as you learn to do in **Part 4**. The wizard just helps you get started.

① Click the name of the style you want formatted for the links in your Hot List.

② Click **Next**.

Importing Links
When you have more experience creating Web pages, you may choose the fourth item, **Import from Web Page**. This item copies a list of links from another page.

Task 5: Choosing the Information About You to Include

Start Here

The Personal Home Page Wizard can include a variety of different sections, listing information about you. You choose which sections to include.

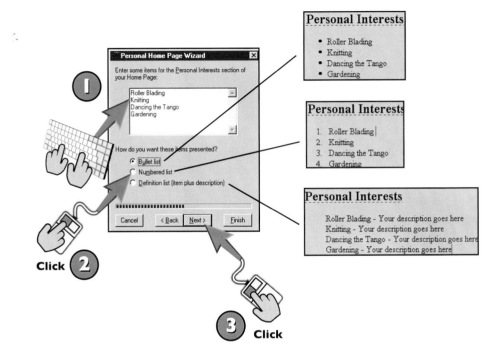

✓ Differentiating List Types

Bullet list style lists each of the items in your list as a "bullet" character, Numbered list numbers each item from one up, and Definition list indents your list and creates extra space following each item for a description, which you can type later.

✓ The Wizard Isn't the Final Word

When you're done with the wizard, you can edit, expand, or enhance your page any way you like. So don't worry too much about the choices you make at this point.

Click (2)

(3) Click

1 Type a list of personal interests in the white box, and press **Enter** after every entry. You can enter as many items as you like.

2 Choose how you want the list displayed by selecting one of the option buttons: **Bullet List**, **Numbered List**, or **Definition List**.

3 Click **Next**.

End Task

Task 6: Putting Contact Information at the Bottom of Your Page

Click

Click

Often, a Web page is intended to provide not one-way communication, but a two-way dialogue. You have something to tell your visitors, but you also want to hear back from them—feedback. That's where adding contact information comes in.

✅ **Checking Check Boxes**
To add a check mark to an empty check box, point to the box and click. To remove a check mark from a check box, point to the box and click.

✅ **Keeping Your Private Information Private!**
On a business Web page, it's often appropriate to include a postal address and a telephone number. But for privacy's sake, never put your home phone number or mailing address on a Web page. Anyone who wants to contact you may do so by email.

① Review the list of check boxes and decide what Contact Information you want to use so that your visitors can contact you.

② Change the check boxes so that check marks appear only next to items you want to include. For practice, let's just select **E-mail Address** and **URL Address**.

③ Click **Next**.

Task 7: Choosing How to Receive Feedback from Your Visitors

Start Here

As the last selection, you now need to decide how you would like feedback sent to you from your visitors. You can use forms, which the visitor fills out, and their comments are either stored in a Web page or in a data file. You can then review their comments later. Or, you can choose to have comments emailed to you directly.

Click

Click

1 Select the method of feedback. For the purposes of this task, choose **Use link, Send E-mail to This Address**.

2 Enter your email address in the text box.

3 Click **Next**.

End Task

Start Here

Task 8: Choosing the Order of Information on Your Page

We're almost there, but first you must decide what order you want for each of the sections you created previously to be listed on your Web page.

Click

Click

3 **Click**

1 Click the Web page section name whose position you want to change.

2 To move the item higher on the page, click **Up**. To move the item lower on the page, click **Down**.

3 When the sections are in the order you want, click **Next**.

End Task

Task 9: Producing the Web Page

After making all your choices, you now must tell the wizard to put the selections together and show them to you.

Click

Click

Click

Click

1 If you want to review your choices, click **Back**.

2 Make any changes you want, then click **Next** until you return to the final dialog box.

3 Click **Finish**. The page appears in FrontPage Express, where you can make additional changes and test it.

Task 10: Saving the New Page

Click

Click

Click

If you have any experience in other creative programs—such as word processors—you know how important it is to save your files. Web page files are no different. You should save your Web page right after creating it, and then again anytime you make changes to it.

✓ **Saving to Specific Folders**
To save the file in a specific folder (for example, Web Pages, as used in previous examples), click the drop-down arrow next to the **Save In** box, at the top of the Save As File dialog box. Locate the **Web Pages** (or whatever you called yours) folder and click it. Then click **Save**.

① Click **File**, and then choose **Save**.

② Click **As File**.

③ Choose a folder to save the Web file in and click **Save**.

✓ **Saving Again Is Even Easier**
After the first time you save a file, you'll no longer need to perform steps 2 and 3 when you save again. Simply performing step 1 saves the file.

Task 11: Closing and Re-Opening a Page File

As you create your Web pages, you'll probably end up making changes as you go along. So, you'll need to open existing files, and then save and close them when you're done.

Click

Click

FrontPage Prompts You to Save

If you did not save your changes before telling FrontPage Express to close the file, a message displays asking if you want to save your changes. Click **Yes**. FrontPage saves your file and then closes it. So you don't have to worry about exiting the program and losing changes.

To close a Web page (without closing FrontPage Express), click **File** and choose **Close**.

To open a Web page you've used recently, click **File**, and then choose the filename from the bottom of the File menu.

Task 12: Opening a Web Page You Haven't Used Lately

If a file you want to edit is not among the files you've worked with recently, its name won't appear on the File menu. In that case, here's how to open any Web page file on your PC.

① Click **File** and choose **Open**.

② Click **Browse**.

③ Use the **Look In** list to navigate to the folder where you stored the Web page.

④ From the Open File dialog box, choose the filename and click **Open**.

Task 13: Changing Your Web Page Title

The real "title" of your Web page does not appear within the layout of the page itself. It appears in the title bar of the browser through which the page is viewed, although Web authors often duplicate the title as a big bold heading at the top of the page. The title is important because it identifies your page in search tools like Yahoo! and in visitor bookmark lists.

Click

Click

✓ **Keeping Your Title Snappy**

Make your title short, but clear and descriptive. In the example, it's clear that this is a personal home page for someone named Harriet. There are probably few sites with that name, but you never know. So, choose your title wisely.

① Open the Web page in FrontPage Express.

② Click **File** and choose **Page Properties**.

③ Click in the **Title** box on the **General** tab and change the title.

Task 14: Starting a Completely Blank Page

Click

Click

Click

Click

Now that you know how to create a basic page using the wizard, it's time to learn how to start one from scratch. It really doesn't matter which way you start—what matters is that you know about both methods, so you can choose the one you need.

Click

(1) Click **File** and choose **New**.

(2) Click **Normal Page** and then click **OK**.

(3) Start typing and formatting the contents of the page, as you learn to do in upcoming parts of this book.

(4) Save your Web page early and often.

✓ **Form Options**
Some of the other choices on the New dialog box—Confirmation Form, Form Page Wizard, and Survey Form—all help you add interactive *forms* to your Web site that your visitors can use to answer questions or provide feedback. (See Part 6, "Creating Tables and Forms," for more information about forms.)

Task 15: Checking Out Your New Page in a Web Browser

Now we're ready to see the results of your first masterpiece in a browser. In FrontPage Express, your Web pages will appear pretty much the same as they do when viewed through a browser. However, it's a good idea to preview your page through your Web browser from time to time to evaluate its appearance.

Start Here

1

Click

2

Click

3

Click

✓ **Locating Your File**
Task 10 suggested saving your Web page files in the Web Pages folder, so you may find the Web file there.

1 In FrontPage Express, click **File** and choose **Exit**.

2 Open your browser without connecting to the Internet, click **File**, and then select **Open**.

3 Click **Browse**.

Next Step

4 Locate and select your Web page.

5 Click **Open**.

6 Click **OK**.

7 Voila! There's your Web page. You can now click the links to test them.

Making Your Page Say What You Want

The main purpose of creating a Web page is to share information with your viewers. And to do that, you need to make the information understandable, right? That means using text to share that information. Yes, you will use pictures or other objects as well, but the efficient use of text is the key to making your Web page say what you want.

In this part, you explore the ways you create, edit, and format Web page text in a Web authoring program. You'll find that the job is very much like using a word processor.

Tasks

Task 1: Selecting Text

To perform most activities involving text, such as changing the style of text or replacing text with different text, you must first select, or *highlight*, the text you want to work with. You select text in FrontPage Express in the same way you select text in most other word-processing programs.

Start Here

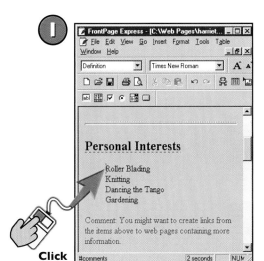

Click

✓ **Understanding Formatting Types**

There are two basic kinds of formatting: paragraph formatting (changing the appearance of whole paragraphs) and character formatting (changing the appearance only of selected characters). When applying character formatting, you must select precisely the characters you want to format. But when applying paragraph formatting, you need only select part of the paragraph. If any part of it is highlighted, any paragraph formatting you apply affects the whole paragraph.

Drag

 For practice, open the Web page you created in Part 2 and point to the beginning of the text that you want to select.

2 Click and drag to highlight the selection: Drag to the right to select all or part of a line; drag down to select multiple lines.

End Task

Task 2: Changing Text on a Page

Click

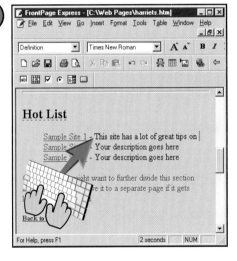

If you used the **Personal Home Page Wizard** to build your first Web page, you have a lot of sample text in your page that you need to replace with text of your own. Even if you did not use the wizard, replacing text is an essential editing skill.

Select the text you want to change.

Type your new text.

✅ **Overwriting Existing Text**
Anything you type automatically replaces the selected text. The new text usually picks up the formatting of the text you are replacing.

Task 3: Typing New Text

In addition to replacing text, you'll need to add new text.

Click

Enter

✓ **Saving Early, Saving Often**

Don't forget to save your Web page file often, especially after adding or changing text.

1 Point to the spot on the page where you want to add new text, and click. The *edit cursor*, a flashing vertical bar, appears where you clicked.

2 Type your text. When you reach the end of a line, just keep typing; the edit cursor jumps automatically to the beginning of the next line.

3 To end a paragraph and start a new one, press **Enter**.

Task 4: Typing Symbols and Special Characters

There will be times when you need characters that don't appear on your keyboard, such as the copyright symbol or accented characters used in other languages. For such occasions, FrontPage Express offers its **Symbol** menu.

Click

Click

Click

Click

Click

1. Point to the spot in the text where you want to insert the character and click to position the edit cursor there.

2. Click **Insert**, then choose **Symbol**.

3. Click the symbol you want to insert. After you click it, it appears next to the **Insert** button.

4. Click **Insert** to insert the character. Click **Close**.

✓ **Reviewing Your Symbols After Font Changes**

If you change the font (as you learn to do in Task 14) of text containing symbols, check the symbols carefully, and re-apply them if necessary. Sometimes changing fonts changes the way symbols appear.

Task 5: Deleting Text

OK, so you did a brain dump and now need to do a little tweaking. Not a problem. You can remove text and start again, if needed.

Drag

Drop

① Select the text you want to delete.

② Press the **Delete** key.

Task 6: Fixing Mistakes

Click

Oops! Maybe you deleted something you didn't mean to in Task 5. If you delete text and then suddenly realize that you want it back, you can use the steps in this task to recover the deleted text. The catch, however, is that you must perform these steps immediately after the mistake; if you perform another action in the meantime, you'll undo *that* action instead of undoing the earlier mistake.

✓ Undoing Several Actions

If you make several changes that you end up not wanting, you can't use undo to fix them. However, you can reverse those mistakes by closing the file without saving it (click **File**, then choose **Close**). The only problem with this method is that you undo not only the mistakes, but *everything* you did to the page since the last time you saved it, possibly including some good stuff you'll then have to redo.

1 Perform any action in FrontPage Express, such as deleting some text.

2 Click **Edit**, then choose **Undo Clear**.

3 Deleted text reappears. If you change your mind again, and want to *undo* the undo (putting the page back the way it was right after Step I), click **Edit** and choose **Redo Clear**.

Task 7: Copying Text

If you have a block of text you want to use in more than one place on your page, there is no need to type it over and over. You can simply type it once and then copy it wherever you need it.

Click

Click

Click

✓ **Repeating a Copy Operation**

After step 4, you can move ahead to other editing activities, or you can copy the same text you selected in step 1 again—and as many more times as you want—by repeating steps 3 and 4 for each copy you want to make.

① Select the text you want to copy.

② Click the **Copy** button on the Standard toolbar.

③ Point to the spot where you want to copy the text and click to position the edit cursor there.

④ Click the **Paste** button on the Standard toolbar. The text appears.

End Task

Task 8: Moving Text

Click

Click

Click

Moving text is really just like copying—except that you don't leave the original text behind. You *cut* it from one place, then *copy* it in another.

1. Select the text you want to move.

2. Click the **Cut** button on the Standard toolbar.

3. Point to the spot where you want to move the text, and click to position the edit cursor there.

4. Click the **Paste** button on the Standard toolbar. The text appears.

✓ **Repeating a Paste Operation**
Just like copying, after moving text you can paste as many copies as you want of the text you cut in step 2. Just repeat steps 3 and 4 for each copy you need.

Task 9: Choosing the Style of a Paragraph

Start Here

The most important part of controlling the appearance of text is choosing the text's **paragraph style** from the Change Style list. There are many styles, but the most important are the six **Heading styles** (Heading 1 is the largest, Heading 6 is the smallest), **Normal style** (used for ordinary paragraphs), and the **List styles** (which you'll meet in Task 12).

✓ **Formatting Paragraphs with Styles**
Paragraph styles are an example of paragraph formatting (not character formatting), so you do not need to highlight the whole paragraph. Select any part of the paragraph, or just put the edit cursor anywhere within the paragraph, and the style you choose will be applied to the entire paragraph.

✓ **Applying Styles to Several Paragraphs**
To apply a style to multiple, consecutive paragraphs at the same time, click anywhere in the first paragraph and drag down to the last paragraph. Then choose your style.

Click

Click

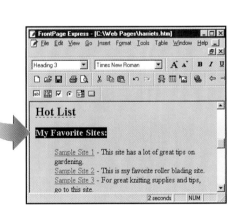

1. Select the paragraph for which you want to change the style.

2. Locate the **Change Style** list box at the left end of the Formatting toolbar. (Notice that it shows the style currently applied to the selected paragraph.)

3. Click the arrow on the right side of the list box to open the list.

4. Click the name of the style you want to apply.

End Task

Task 10: Indenting a Paragraph

Start Here

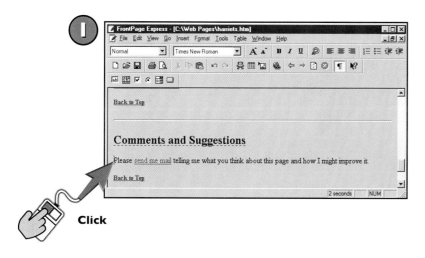

Click

To *indent* is to push text inward from the margin, in order to make it stand out on the page and to better show that the indented text is a part of the heading or other text above it. Indenting selected paragraphs can give your Web page structure and uniformity.

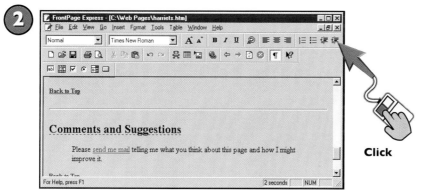

Click

1 Place your cursor on the first line of a single paragraph or select multiple paragraphs that you want to indent.

2 Click the **Increase Indent** button on the Formatting toolbar.

✔ **Increasing the Indent**
To indent farther, click the **Increase Indent** button multiple times.

✔ **Decreasing the Indent**
To remove the indent, click the **Decrease Indent** button on the Formatting toolbar.

End Task

Task 11: Lining Up Paragraphs on the Left, Right, or in the Center

You can *align* in three ways: flush to the left side of the page (left alignment), centered on the page (center alignment), or flush to the ride side (right alignment).

Click

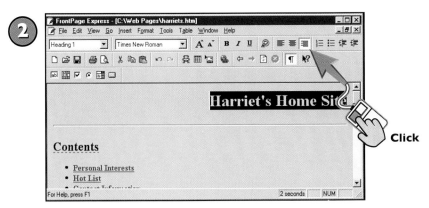

Click

Choosing Paragraph Alignment

Most of the time, left alignment is best, especially for Normal-style paragraphs. Center can be nice for large headings (such as Heading 1 or Heading 2 style), especially if not used too much. Save right alignment for special needs.

1. Select the paragraph or paragraphs you want to align.

2. Click one of the three alignment buttons on the Formatting toolbar: **Align Left**, **Center**, or **Align Right**.

Task 12: Creating Lists

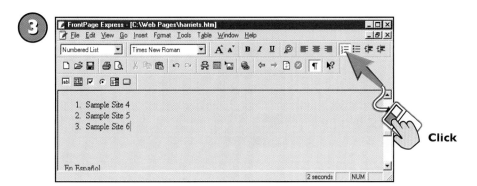

Click

There are two types of ordered lists: numbered and bulleted. (You can also create an unordered list, but it's far less interesting.) In a *numbered list*, the list items are preceded by consecutive numbers. In a *bulleted list*, each item in the list is preceded by a symbol, a bullet character. Lists are a great way to organize and present content in an easy-to-read fashion.

✔ **Formatting Lists**
List formatting is paragraph formatting, so you can select a list by starting the selection anywhere in the first item, then dragging down to anywhere in the last item.

✔ **Choosing a List Type**
When the order of the items in the list is important, as in step-by-step instructions, use a numbered list. When the order doesn't matter, use a bulleted list.

① Type the list items, pressing **Enter** after each so that each list item is on a separate line.

② Select the entire list.

③ Click one of the two list buttons on the Formatting toolbar: **Numbered List** or **Bulleted List**.

End Task

Task 13: Choosing (or Changing) the Style of a List

Creating a list involves just a click of a button. But, you don't have to settle for what you get. You can easily modify the appearance of a list, choose a different numbering style (A B C, I II III, and so on), or select a different bullet style.

Start Here

Click

Click

Click

Click

(1) Select the list.

(2) Click **Format**, then choose **Bullets and Numbering**.

(3) Click the new style you want to use from the options shown.

(4) Click **OK**. The list appears in the new style.

End Task

Task 14: Choosing a Font for Text

The best way to control the style of text is to choose the appropriate paragraph style, as you did in Task 9. But beyond the styles, you can dress up text even more by choosing a different font.

✓ Applying Fonts
Fonts are a form of character formatting, not paragraph formatting, so they affect only the exact characters you select. In order to apply a font to a whole paragraph, you must select the whole paragraph. The same is true of the character formatting you discover in Tasks 15, 16, and 17.

✓ Choosing Common Fonts
Some browsers don't support various, nonstandard fonts. If you use nonstandard fonts, the browsers still see your text, but they won't see it in its original style. Some standard fonts like Arial and Times New Roman are usually safe.

1 Select the exact characters you want to apply a new font to.

2 Locate the **Change Font** list box in the Formatting toolbar. Notice that the box tells the name of the font that's now used for the selected text.

3 Click the arrow on the right side of the list box to open the list.

4 Click the name of the font you want to apply. The text appears in the new font.

Task 15: Making Text Bigger or Smaller

The paragraph style determines size. For example, if text set in Heading 3 style looks too small to you, the best solution is to change it to a bigger style, such as Heading 2 or Heading 1. However, you can fine-tune the size of selected text easily when the size chosen by the style isn't exactly what you want.

✔ **Changing Text Size by Larger Increments**
You can click the **Increase Text Size** or **Decrease Text Size** buttons multiple times to make text bigger or smaller. For example, to make text two levels bigger, click the **Increase Text Size** button twice.

✔ **Text Size Has Limits**
If you click **Increase Text Size** and the selected text does not get any bigger, the text is already set at the largest size allowed. Similarly, if **Decrease Text Size** does nothing, the text is already set at the minimum size allowed.

Click

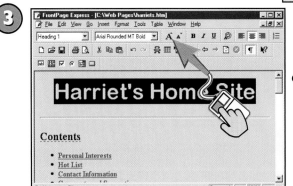

Click

1 Select the exact characters you want to make bigger or smaller.

2 Locate the two buttons to the right of the Change Font list on the Formatting toolbar.

3 To make the selected text larger, click the **Increase Text Size** button. To make the selected text smaller, click the **Decrease Text Size** button.

Start Here

Task 16: Making Text Bold, Italic, or Underlined

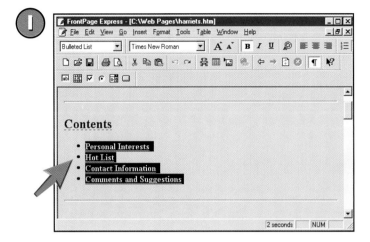

Text and paragraph formatting, and the fonts you use are all important. However, **bold**, *italic* and underlining are valuable tools also. They are great for emphasis or for making text match editorial standards (such as setting book titles in italics). Though valuable tools, use them sparingly—overuse can make text busy and hard to read.

Click

(✓) Removing Formatting
To remove bold, italic, or underlining, select the text and click the button again. For example, to remove bolded formatting, select it and click the **Bold** button.

(✓) Combining Formatting Types
You can combine these kinds of formatting; for example, you can make the selected text both bold and italic by clicking the **Bold** button, then the **Italic** button.

(1) Select the exact characters you want to format.

(2) Locate the group of three buttons to the right of the Decrease Text Size button on the Formatting toolbar.

(3) Click the **Bold**, **Italic**, or **Underline** buttons to format the selected characters.

End Task

Task 17: Choosing the Color of Text

In Part 5, you learn how to choose a coordinated color scheme for your Web page—a scheme for making sure that all the colors used for text, background, and other objects all work together. If you do that, you probably won't choose colors selectively for blocks of text. Still, you might want to give a heading or other selected text unique color.

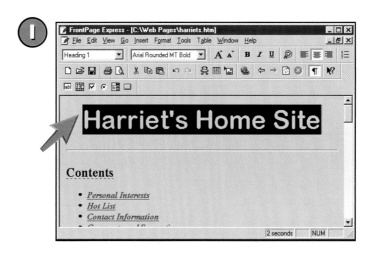

✓ Creating Custom Text Colors

If none of the colors that appear in the Color dialog box appeal to you, click the **Define Custom Colors** button. A palette displays, showing all the colors that are possible on your PC, as it is currently configured. Click the palette to create a Custom color, then apply that color by clicking the square in which it appears.

Click

1 Select the exact characters you want to choose a color for.

2 Click the **Text Color** button on the Formatting toolbar.

Next Step

3 Click the colored square containing the color you want to apply. (Be careful to choose a color that will show up against the current background color.) Click **OK**.

4 The text appears in the new color.

Making Links

Links are the lifelines of the Web. They can be used to connect visitors to other areas on a single Web page or to separate pages. They also do other stuff, such as begin to download files. Without links, the Web wouldn't be. And even though links sound a little complicated, they are extremely easy to create. The hardest part is deciding where you want a link to lead.

Tasks

Task 1: Exploring How Links Work

Every link has two parts: the *link source*—the object in the page that a visitor clicks to activate the link—and the *URL*—the address of the page to which the link takes the visitor. Creating links is really just a matter of creating the link source in your page, then adding the URL behind it. You can learn a lot more about links by studying the link sources and URLs on the pages you visit online.

Click

✓ Spotting Links

When the link source is text, it usually appears underlined and in a unique color. When the link source is a picture, you can locate the link by pointing to the picture; if it's a link, the pointer becomes a pointing hand.

1 Open your Web browser (Internet Explorer or Netscape Navigator) and connect to the Internet.

2 Surf to a page you like that contains links.

Right-Click

Click

(3) Point to a link, in which the link source is text, and right-click it.

(4) Choose **Properties**. The Properties dialog box shows the address (URL) to which the link points, along with other information.

✅ **Copying a Web Address**
You can copy a Web page address from the Properties dialog box by selecting the address, then right-clicking and choosing Copy. If you then go immediately to FrontPage Express to create a link in a page, you can paste the URL into the dialog box by clicking there and pressing Ctrl+V.

Task 2: Choosing Where the Links in Your Personal Page Point

Start Here

If you used FrontPage Express's Personal Home Page Wizard to start a page (as described in Part 2), then your page already contains some links: the Hot List. But those links lead to phony addresses now. Here's how to make them point wherever you want.

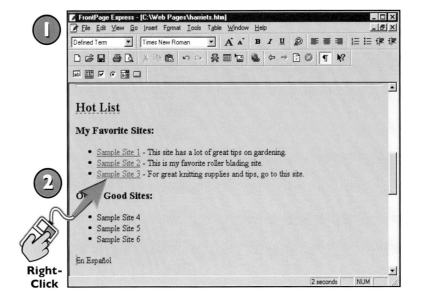

Right-Click

✓ **Editing the Link Source**

You can, of course, edit the link source to change it from Sample Site to anything you like. But sometimes when you edit link source text, you inadvertently remove the link formatting—you change it from a link source to ordinary text. If that happens, just re-create the link, as described in the first few steps of Task 3. It only takes a couple of clicks.

1 Decide on a Web site address you like. (If you need a suggestion, try **http://www.mcp.com**.)

2 Point to one of the Sample Site links listed in your Hot List. Right-click the **Sample Site** link.

Next Step

Click

Click

Click

3 Choose **Hyperlink Properties**.

4 Be sure that the **World Wide Web** tab is selected.

5 In the box labeled **URL**, type the complete URL. Be sure to include the **http://** part at the beginning.

6 Click **OK**. The link source you pointed to in step 2 is now a link that points to the URL you chose.

✅ **Always Ask Permission to Link**
Before publishing a page that contains links to other Web sites, visit those Web sites and look for the email address of the person responsible for the site: the Webmaster. As a courtesy, email the Webmaster to ask if it's OK to publish a link to the site.

End Task

Task 3: Creating New Links from Scratch

In Task 2, you had a head start because the link source had already been created, so all you had to do was add the URL. Now it's time to create a link from scratch: source and URL together.

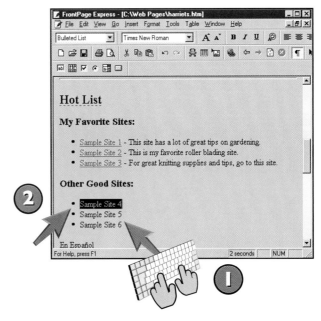

Formatting Links
Although you can apply character formatting (such as fonts or italics) to the link source text you create, it's best not to. Browsers usually display link source text with standard formatting (usually blue and underlined) to help the visitor instantly identify links on a page. You don't want your character formatting to make finding links tricky for your visitors by changing the link source formatting they're accustomed to seeing.

Click

1 Type and format the text that will serve as the link source.

2 Select the text.

3 Click the **Create or Edit Hyperlink** button on the Standard toolbar.

Click

④ Be sure that the **World Wide Web** tab is selected.

⑤ In the box labeled **URL**, type the complete URL. Be sure to include the **http://** part at the beginning. Click **OK**.

⑥ The selected text becomes a hyperlink.

Task 4: Linking Your Own Pages to Each Other to Make a Web Site

Ultimately, you might have more to say than can fit conveniently on a single page. So, you'll need to create a *Web site* made up of several pages that link together. Linking one of your own pages to other pages is a little different from linking elsewhere—but still easy.

Start Here

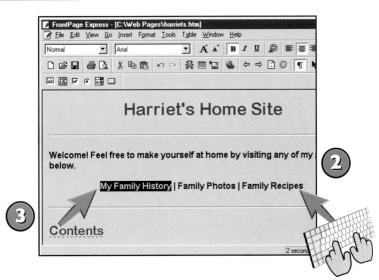

✔ Creating a Navigation Menu

One good way to link pages together is to create a string of links, containing a separate link for each page, and placing them at the bottom of every page. That way, your visitors can jump from any page in your Web site to any other, with just one click.

Create the Web pages that will make up your Web site and save them all in the same folder.

② Type and format the text that will serve as the link sources.

③ Select the text of one link source.

Next Step

Click

Click

Don't Believe the Type
When typing your page filename in the **URL** box, ignore the entry in the **Hyperlink Type** box. That entry automatically becomes **Other** when you click **OK**, which is what you want.

Store All the Files Together!
When you publish this Web site, it will be important that you store all your Web page files in the same directory on the Web server.

4. Click the **Create or Edit Hyperlink** button on the Standard toolbar.

5. Be sure that the **World Wide Web** tab is selected.

6. In the box labeled **URL**, type the complete filename of the Web page you are linking to (including the **.htm** part). Do not put http:// or anything else at the beginning.

7. Click **OK**.

Links don't always lead to other pages or files. In a long or complex page, a link might lead to another part of the same page. If you created the Personal Home Page in Part 2, you might have noticed that the top of the page contains a Contents list of links, each of which jumps to a particular section of the page. That Contents list works because of *bookmarks*, such as the following ones that you are about to create.

✓ **Using the Default Bookmark Name**
In step 3, the text you selected in step 1 appears automatically as the bookmark name. You can leave that text alone and let it serve as the name, or change it to another name. Changing the bookmark name has no effect on the text in the page.

Task 5: Linking to a Particular Spot on a Page

Start Here

Click

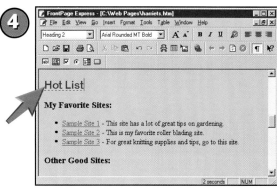

Click

① Select text at the spot where you want a bookmark.

② Click **Edit**, then choose **Bookmark**.

③ Type a name for the bookmark and click **OK**.

④ Create the link source for a link to that bookmark.

Next Step

Click

Click

Click

Click

Click

5 Select the link source, then click the **Create or Edit Hyperlink** button on the Standard toolbar.

6 Click the **Open Pages** tab.

7 Click the **Bookmark** drop-down list and choose the bookmark name.

8 Click **OK**.

You might have content that you want to offer your visitors, but don't want to turn into a Web page—for example, if you have a lengthy document, report, or other file. In that case, it might be better to provide that file for downloading instead of turning it into a Web page (or series of Web pages). You can provide any kind of computer file for downloading—documents, sound clips, pictures, and so on.

✅ Using Helper Programs

To use a file you provide, the visitor must have the same program. For example, if you publish a Word file, the visitor must have a program that can display (or convert) Word files to view it. You cannot do much about this, except to try to offer only popular, widely used file types, such as Word for documents, .avi for video clips (see Part 5), or .wav for sound clips.

Task 6: Linking to Files So Your Visitors Can Download Them

Locate the file you want to link to and move or copy it to the folder where your Web page files are stored.

In the Web page, type and format the text that you want to use as the link source.

Select the text of the link source.

Click

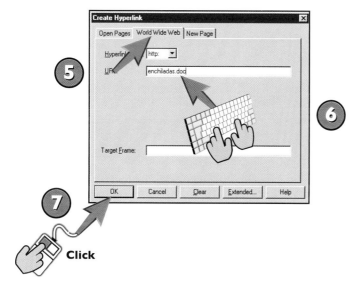

Click

✅ **Always Provide the File Type and Size**
In the link source text (or right next to it), it's courteous to tell your visitors the file type so they can tell whether it's a file they are equipped to view. Providing the size of the file is also a good idea. That way, your viewers can guesstimate how long it will take to download at the speed of their Internet connection.

④ Click the **Create or Edit Hyperlink** button on the Standard toolbar.

⑤ Be sure that the **World Wide Web** tab is selected.

⑥ In the box labeled **URL**, type the complete filename of the file. Do not put "http://" at the beginning.

⑦ Click **OK**.

✅ **Did We Mention Storing the Files Together?**
When you publish this Web site, it is important that you store all your Web page files in the same directory on the Web server.

Near the bottom of the **Personal Home Page** example, and in many pages you see online, a *signature* appears. A signature is text telling visitors who created (or manages) the page. Usually, a signature includes a *mailto* link, a link that points to the email address of the Web page author. If you add a signature and mailto link to your page, when a visitor clicks that link, his email program opens a new message, automatically preaddressed to you.

Task 7: Linking to Your Email So Visitors Can Contact You

Click

Near the bottom of your page (or in another easy-to-find spot), type a signature message such as the one shown.

Select some text in the message—your name or email address—to serve as a link source for the mailto link.

Click the **Create or Edit Hyperlink** button on the Standard toolbar and be sure that the **World Wide Web** tab is selected.

Click

④ In the box labeled **URL**, type your complete email address. Do not put http:// or anything else at the beginning.

⑤ In the Hyperlink Type box, choose **mailto:**. The word mailto appears right before your email address.

⑥ Click **OK**. The text becomes a mailto: link.

✔️ Naming Your Mailto Link

The link source of a mailto link need not show your exact email address, because most visitor email programs will use the correct address automatically when they click the link. However, some visitors use Internet software that doesn't support mailto links; they see the link source, but nothing happens when they click it. So always include your exact email address somewhere in the signature.

Task 8: Checking That Links Go Where They're Supposed To

When you create links that lead from your page to other pages online, the only way to be absolutely sure that links lead where they're supposed to is to test the links online—after you've published your page. However, you can do a pretty reliable prepublishing link check at any time, right from within FrontPage Express.

Click

Click

✓ **You Can Test Your Links Offline...**
You don't need to connect to the Internet to test links to bookmarks or to files on your PC (such as other pages within a Web site you're creating but have not yet published). You can test those just by opening the page file in your browser and trying the links offline.

① Connect to the Internet, open FrontPage Express, and open the page file in which you want to test the links.

② Point to a link you want to test and click so that the edit cursor appears there.

③ Click **Tools**, then choose **Follow Hyperlink**.

Next Step

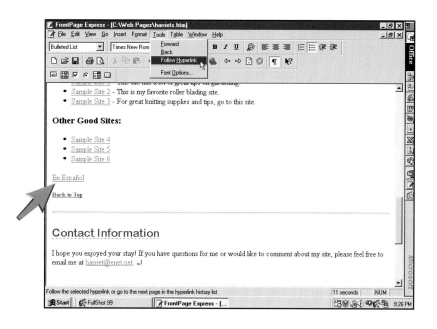

4 Be sure to test the other links on your page.

 ...But Test Them Again Online
Even if your links work, be certain to test them again, online, after you have published your page.

Adding Style to Your Pages

Most of the hard stuff is over—filling your Web pages with text. Now comes the fun and creative part. In this part, you can explore unique ways to give your page style, including choosing colors, adding pictures, and even adding animation and sound.

One word of caution, though—a busy, over-styled Web page is an eyesore. Less is truly more in the case of Web design. Most visitors hit a page for its content, not its style. Although style is a nice addition, if it overwhelms the substance, you might lose more visitors than you gain. But that doesn't mean you can't be creative.

Colors, backgrounds, and horizontal lines help a page's appeal; there really is no impact on page's performance. However, every picture, sound, or animation you add to a page lengthens the time it takes the page to fully materialize on a visitor's screen. You know from your own surfing trips how frustrating a slow Web page is, especially when it's slow because it has too many pictures. So, my advice is to use style conservatively so as not to overdo it.

Tasks

To add appeal, you can choose a *color scheme*, a group of colors that both contrast and complement one another. In creating your scheme, you pick the color for the background, text, links, *visited links* (links the visitor has used already), and *active links* (links the visitor has just clicked, but which still appear onscreen briefly while the link is being activated).

✔️ **Jazzing Up Your Background**
Instead of a solid color background, you can use an image as a background (see Task 16).

✔️ **Ensuring Good Contrast**
Be careful that all your selected text and link colors stand out against the background. For example, if you select a dark background color, all the text colors must be light so that the text will be legible. You can adjust all these options from the Background tab.

Task 1: Choosing Text Colors and Background Colors

Open a Web page for which you want to choose colors.

Click **File**, and then choose **Page Properties**.

Click the **Background** tab.

Click

Click

Click

4 Click the arrow on the **Background** drop-down list to display your color options.

5 Click the color you want to use for the background.

6 Repeat steps 4 and 5 for the other color lists. Click **OK**.

✅ Allowing Default Colors

Choosing Default from a color list assigns no color. It allows the color for that object to be determined by the color settings in the visitor's browser. Because the color the browser chooses might not show up properly with other colors you've selected, never pick Default unless you pick Default for all colors in the page.

✅ Creating Custom Colors

In the color lists, the Custom choice opens a dialog box from which you can create and select a different color from those already shown in the list.

Task 2: Adding Lines to Divide Up a Page

Horizontal lines help to visually divide up a page. Used between a heading and the paragraph that follows it, a line can add a little extra style to page. Lines also help divide sections of a longer page.

Using Fancier Lines
You might see fancy, multicolor lines dividing some pages. These aren't real lines; they're pictures, used like lines. You can find these pictures in clip art libraries (see Task 4) in categories with names like Bars or Rules, and you insert them like any other picture (see Task 8).

 Click on the page where you want to insert the line.

 Click **Insert**, then choose **Horizontal Line**. The line appears on your page.

Task 3: Changing the Look of a Line

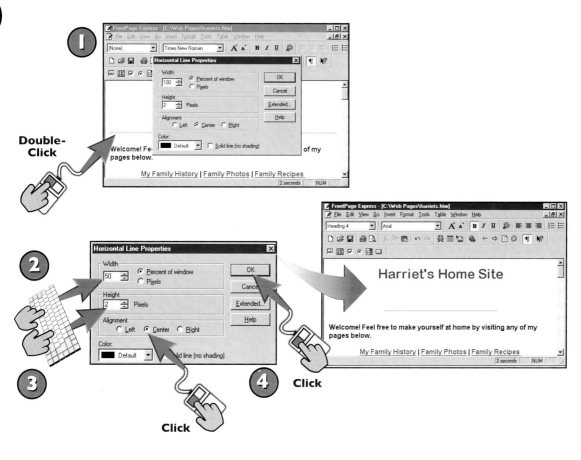

Double-Click

Click

Click

Click

Now that you have a horizontal line in place, you can change its appearance by making it thicker, thinner, shorter, or changing its alignment on the page.

① Double-click a line.

② To make the line shorter than the full width of the page, in **Width** type a percentage figure less than 100.

③ In **Height**, type a number to change the thickness of the line; a higher number makes a thicker line.

④ Select the Alignment (**Left**, **Right**, or **Center**) you want, the line **Color**, and click **OK**.

✅ Determining Line Width

In the Horizontal Line Properties dialog box, always leave the **Percent of Window** option selected, so that the number you type in **Width** expresses the width as a percentage of the page's width. Choosing the other option might produce unpredictable results on visitor screens.

End Task

Nearly all the images you see on Web pages are in the GIF file type. Some images are in JPEG format, mostly photographs. But any pictures used in your Web pages must be in one of these two formats. You can create your own pictures (see Task 6), but you can also pick up great pictures from clip art libraries on CD or online.

✓ Paying the Clip Art Piper
Some clip art you must pay for, some is free, and some is free with strings attached. Always read and follow all copyright notices and other usage instructions on any page from which you download clip art or other files you plan to use.

✓ Locating Clip Art Treasures
A good way to find tons of clip art sites is to do a search with Yahoo! (www.yahoo.com), Excite (www.excite.com) or another search page, using **Web Clip Art** as a search term.

Task 4: Finding Pictures

Click

1 In your Web browser, go to a good online clip art library or site. If you don't know which one to choose, use **www.clipartconnection.com** for starters.

2 Click through the categories to locate an image you want to use.

Task 5: Copying a Picture from the Web

**Right-
Click**

Click

Click

Click

When you locate a clip art
picture online that you
want to use, you can copy it
to a folder on your PC
(shown in the following
steps), and use it later to
insert on your Web pages
(as shown in Task 8).

✓ Using CD-ROM Clip Art

If the picture you want to
use is in a clip art library
you obtained on a floppy
disk or CD-ROM, always
copy the picture file from
there to the folder where
your Web page files are
stored, and then insert the
picture as shown in Task 8.

① While viewing the clip art in your browser, right-click the picture.

② Choose **Save Picture As** (if you browse in Internet Explorer) or **Save Image As**
(if you browse in Netscape Navigator).

③ Open the **Save In** list and choose the folder that contains your Web page files.

④ Click **Save**.

Task 6: Creating Pictures

Start Here

You can create your own Web page pictures with almost any draw or paint program you might have. In fact, **Paint**—the program built into **Windows**—works perfectly for beginners.

✓ **Learning More About Paint**

To learn how to paint a picture in Windows Paint, open Paint, click **Help**, and click **Help Topics**.

✓ **Using Your Own Pictures**

To get your own photographs into your Web pages, scan them with a scanner, take them to a computer graphics shop to be scanned, or take them with a digital camera. Use the scanner or camera software to save the image as a **GIF** or **JPEG** file and store it in the same folder as your other Web page files. You can even have picture disks created when you get your film developed.

Click Start, then choose **Programs**, **Accessories**, and **Paint**.

Use Paint's tools to create your masterpiece.

When you are finished creating your masterpiece, be sure to save it. Click **File**, then choose **Save**.

Next Step

Click

Click

(4) Use the **Save In** list to select the folder where you store the Web page in which you will use this picture.

(5) Type a short **File Name** for your creation. Don't type a *filename extension* (a period and three letters at the end).

(6) Click the **Save as Type** drop-down list and choose **GIF (*.gif)**.

(7) Click **Save**.

✓ **Converting Other Graphics Formats**
If you use a draw, paint, or scan program that can't optionally save files in GIF or JPEG format, you can still use the picture. FrontPage Express can automatically convert most other common picture file formats— including .BMP, .PCX, and .TIFF—to GIF. Just save in one of those formats and let FrontPage Express handle the conversion.

Task 7: Giving a Picture a Transparent Background

Using your draw, paint, or image-editing software, you can give your GIF pictures a "transparent" background; without a transparent background, the picture appears to have a rectangular, colored background. A transparent background removes the colored rectangle, allowing the page's background to show through. Here's how to choose transparency in Paint.

✓ **Choosing a Transparent Color**
If parts of the picture are the same as the background color, they too become transparent when you perform step 3. To prevent this, between steps 2 and 3, click the **Select Color** button and choose a color not used elsewhere in your picture.

✓ **Viewing the Transparent Color**
After you insert the picture (see Task 8), the background will not look transparent in FrontPage Express. To see your GIF as visitors will see it, view the page through your browser.

Click

Click

Click

Click

(1) In Paint, open a picture you've saved in GIF format.

(2) Click **Image**, then choose **Attributes**.

(3) In the Transparency section, select the check box next to **Use Transparent Background Color**.

(4) Click **OK**.

Task 8: Putting a Picture in a Page

Click

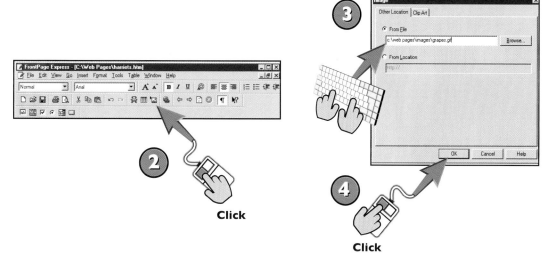

Click

Click

Click

When you have your **GIF** or **JPEG** image ready to go, just drop it in your page, right where you want it. It's important to start with the picture file stored in the same folder as your Web page file. This not only makes inserting the picture easier, but also makes publishing easier when it comes time to publish your Web pages, as you learn in Part 7.

✓ Moving Images
To move a picture after inserting it, just point to it, click and hold, drag to the new spot, and then release. Or, select the picture, click the **Cut** button, click in the new spot, and click the **Paste** button.

✓ Inserting Other Image Formats
If the picture you want to insert is not in **GIF** or **JPEG** format, you can still insert it by typing its filename in step 3. When you save the Web page, FrontPage Express automatically converts the file to **GIF** format.

1. Click in your page at the spot where you want to insert the picture.

2. Click the **Insert Image** button on the Standard toolbar.

3. Type the filename of the picture or click **Browse** to locate it.

4. Click **OK**.

Task 9: Changing the Size of a Picture

After inserting a picture, you can change its size within FrontPage Express.

Start Here

Click

Click & Drag

Click

Resizing Images
When you drag a corner handle, dragging toward the center of the image makes it smaller, and dragging away from the center makes it larger.

(1) Click on the picture to select it. **Handles**—little squares—appear around the picture to show that it is selected.

(2) Point to a handle on a corner—**not** a side or the top or bottom—of the picture.

(3) Click and hold on the corner handle, and drag to resize the image.

(4) Click anywhere else in the page to deselect the picture.

End Task

Task 10: Changing the Shape of a Picture

Click

Click

Click

Click

In Task 9, you were told to only drag the corner handles of an image to resize it. That is because the corner handles automatically resize the height and width proportionately, so that the image retains its basic shape and appearance. However, when working with abstract shapes or going for a special effect, you can drag the handles on the top, bottom, or sides to change the shape of the image, stretching or squeezing (and distorting) it.

① Click on the picture to select it.

② To stretch or squash the picture vertically, drag a top or bottom handle.

③ To widen or narrow the picture horizontally, drag a side handle.

④ Click anywhere else in the page to deselect the picture.

Undoing Mistakes
If you decide you don't like the way you changed the shape of the image, use the **Undo Clear** button to restore the image to its original size and shape.

End Task

Task 11: Putting a Border Around a Picture

To give an image a more polished look, you can put a border around it.

✓ **Selecting Border Size**
Typing "2" in **Border Thickness** makes a simple, bold border. A lower number makes a finer border; a higher number, a thicker one. A border thicker than 10 is probably overkill. A border of 0 is no border at all—some Web sites eliminate the border from images that are used for links.

✓ **Spacing Your Images**
On the Appearance tab, you have boxes for choosing Horizontal Spacing and Vertical Spacing. Raising the numbers in these boxes adds extra space between the image (or the image border, if you've added one) and whatever is next to it. Increasing vertical spacing adds space above and below the image; increasing horizontal spacing adds space to the left and right of the image.

Start Here

Right-Click

Click

Click

Click

① Right-click on the picture.

② Choose **Image Properties**.

③ Click the **Appearance** tab.

④ In **Border Thickness**, type a number to add the border, then click **OK**.

End Task

Task 12: Choosing a Picture's Alignment

Click

Click

By default, any picture you insert goes on the left side of the page. But you can center it or align it to the right side of the page, exactly as you do text.

1. Click on the picture to select it.

2. From the Formatting toolbar, click the **Align Left**, **Center**, or **Align Right** button.

Task 13: Controlling How Text Aligns to a Picture

When you use images around text, you have control of the relationship between the text and picture. You can choose to start text below the image, to the right of it, or to the left of it.

Start Here

Right-Click

Click

Click

Click

Click

Aligning Your Images with Text

There are too many text alignment options to show each one here, but the most important choices are: top (text aligns to the upper-right corner of the image), bottom (text at lower-right corner of the image), middle (text at the middle of the right side of the image), and right (the image goes to the right of the text).

1 Right-click on the picture, and choose **Image Properties**.

2 Click the **Appearance** tab.

3 Click the **Alignment** drop-down list and choose the alignment you want to apply.

4 Click **OK**.

End Task

Task 14: Using a Picture as a Link

1 (Click)

2 Click

3

4 Click

Using a picture as a *link source*—the thing a visitor clicks to activate a link (refer to Part 4)—is just like using text as a link source. The only difference is that you start out by selecting a picture, not text.

① Click on the picture you want to make into a link to select it.

② Click the **Create Hyperlink** button on the Standard toolbar.

③ From the World Wide Web tab, type the URL of the page or file to which this link leads.

④ Click **OK**.

✓ **Using Images as Links**
On the Create Hyperlink dialog box, you can do anything you would do for a text link (refer to Part 4). You can link to files or email addresses (creating a mailto link), or use the Open Pages tab to link to other pages in your Web site or to bookmarks on a page.

Task 15: Creating a Times Square–Style Animated Marquee

A *marquee* is a short slice of animated text that scrolls through a Web page. The effect is like the scrolling marquee on the *New York Times* building in Manhattan, the one people in movies are always watching for bulletins during a crisis. Marquees are a fast way to add a little action to a page and are usually used for text you really want the visitor to notice.

Click

Click

✓ Marquees Are Not Universal

At this writing, scrolling marquees are supported in Internet Explorer, but not in Netscape Navigator. Navigator users will see your marquee text as regular, static text on the page.

1 Click the page at the spot where you want to insert your scrolling marquee.

2 Click **Insert**, and then choose **Marquee**.

3 Type the text you want to see scrolling along.

Next Step

4 You can use the default options for **Direction**, **Speed**, and so on, or make any changes to these settings you desire.

5 Click **OK**. The marquee text appears in FrontPage Express as a fixed, ordinary heading.

6 View the page in Internet Explorer to see the marquee scroll as it will to visitors who use Internet Explorer.

✅ **Changing Text Options**
To change the options or text for a scrolling marquee, just double-click on the marquee to open the **Marquee Properties** dialog box, change whatever you like, and then click **OK**.

Task 16: Adding a Picture Background

Instead of using a solid color background, as you learned to do in Task 1, you can use a picture as a background. If the picture is too small to fill the whole window in which the page appears, it is automatically *tiled*—repeated—to fill the window.

Click

Click

Click

(✓) **Finding Background Images**

You can get background image files that are specially designed so that, when tiled, they form a seamless texture, such as marble or wood. In clip art libraries, look for such images under categories labeled **Backgrounds** or **Textures.** You can also save the background of any Web page you visit by pointing to the background, right-clicking, and choosing the **Save** command from the resulting pop-up menu.

(1) Store the GIF image you want for a background in the same folder as the page you want to use it in.

(2) In FrontPage Express, open the page you want to add a background to, click **File**, and choose **Page Properties**.

(3) Click the **Background** tab.

(4) Click the check box next to **Background Image** to place a check mark there.

Next Step

5 Click in the box beneath Background Image and type the filename of the GIF image you want to use.

6 Click **OK**.

✅ **Images Override Background Colors**
An image background automatically supercedes a background color. If you create an image background, any selection you might have made for background color is irrelevant.

✅ **Keeping Pages Up to Speed**
An image background, like any picture file, slows down the download of your page to the visitor, so watch out for using very large background files. A large background image can slow the page down more than a small, tiled picture.

Task 17: Finding and Adding Animations

A special kind of GIF image file, called an *animated GIF*, plays a brief, simple animation when you view it in a Web page. A good way to find Web sites offering animated GIFs is to do a search with Yahoo (www.yahoo.com), Excite (www.excite.com), or another search page, using animated gif as a search term.

✓ Viewing the Animation
Because FrontPage Express cannot play animated GIFs, you'll have to view it in Internet Explorer to see the animation in action.

✓ Creating Animated GIFs
You can create your own animated GIFs by creating a small series (6–12) of separate GIF images, each of which is a frame of the animation. Then you use a program, such as GIF Construction Set, to combine the frames into one animated GIF.

Start Here

Click

Right-Click

Click

1 In your Web browser, go to a clip art library containing a good selection of animated GIFs, such as the one we used before (www.clipartconnection.com).

2 Click through the categories to locate an animated GIF you want to use.

3 Copy the GIF to your PC and insert it in a Web page exactly as you would any GIF image (refer to Tasks 5 and 8).

End Task

Task 18: Finding Sound Clips

Start Here

Click

A variety of different sound file formats are used on the Web. But for Windows users, the easiest type to deal with is .wav, known as *Wave*. Wave files (and other popular sound-file formats, such as .AU and .MID), are available in sound-clip libraries online or on CD-ROM. You can download sounds to your PC, then use them in your Web pages two ways: as background sounds or as a file to which a link leads, so that a visitor can choose to play the sound by clicking the link.

✓ **Record Your Own Voice Greeting**
Using your PC's sound card and a microphone, you can record your own Wave files. Most sound cards include their own audio recording program.

✓ **Finding Sound Clips**
You can search for sound clips in the same way you search for clip art. Also, sound clips are found on related sites.

1 In your Web browser, go to a sound-clip archive, like those listed here in the Yahoo! directory (**www.yahoo.com**).

2 Click through the categories to locate an image you want to use.

End Task

Task 19: Playing a Background Sound

A background sound is a sound clip that plays automatically when the visitor arrives at the page. You can add a background sound to a page in FrontPage Express, and choose whether that sound should play once, several times, or repeatedly.

Start Here

Click

✅ **Background Sounds Are Not Universal**
At this writing, background sounds are supported in Internet Explorer, but not in Netscape Navigator. So be sure your background sound doesn't contain anything essential to the page, such as a spoken welcome that's not repeated in regular text.

I Get (or create) a short Wave or MIDI file you want to use as a background sound and store it in the same folder in which your Web page files are stored.

2 In FrontPage Express, open the page you want to add the sound to, click **File**, and choose **Page Properties**.

3 Be sure the **General** tab is selected.

Next Step

④ In the Background Sound section of the dialog box, click in the box labeled **Location** and type the filename of the Wave or MIDI file.

⑤ In **Loop**, type the number of times you want the sound to repeat, or check the check box next to **Forever** to make the sound play for as long as the visitor views the page.

⑥ Click **OK**.

✅ **Speak Up!**
Be sure your speakers are on to hear the background sound using Internet Explorer.

✅ **Don't Repeat Yourself**
As a rule, most sound effects or snips of speech are annoying if played more than once, so for these, type 1 in the **Loop** box. Some music clips or other sounds might be nice if kept playing; for them, you can click the **Forever** check box to play the sound continuously.

Creating Tables and Forms

Like word-processing programs, creating Web pages with FrontPage Express offers tools for organizing content in attractive ways: headings, lists, indentation, alignment, horizontal lines, and wrapping around pictures. However, if you need to organize a lot of content (eight or more items) that fall logically into groups, using a table to display the content is the way to go. In this part, you discover not only how to make tables but some nice techniques on how to make them look good, too.

Before you leave this part, you also get an introduction to a technique that doesn't simply organize information, but actually collects it from your visitors: a *form*.

Tasks

Task 1: Inserting a New Table

All you need to get started using tables is a page in progress, a rough idea of what you want to put in the table, and a rough idea of where you want to put it.

✓ **Determining Rows and Columns**

If you are not sure of how many rows and columns you will need, simply guess. You can always add more or remove some later.

✓ **Don't Worry About the Table Borders**

The dashed lines that show the table borders and gridlines appear just to show you where your table is—they don't show up when the page is viewed through a browser. A table without borders still organizes its contents into rows and columns. If you really want visible borders, see Task 5.

✓ **Sizing Rows and Columns**

Don't worry about the size of the rows and columns. As you put text into the cells, the rows and columns will expand to fit whatever you put in them.

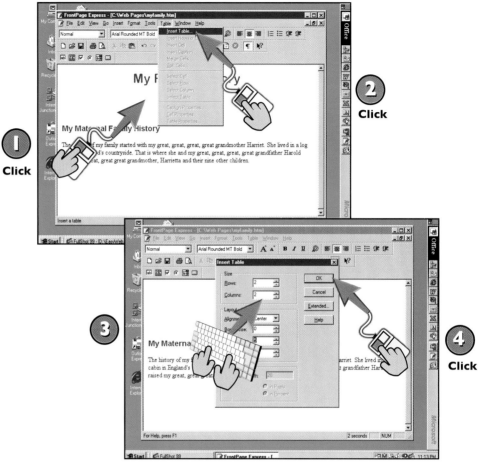

Click the spot in your page where you want to insert the table.

Click **Table**, then choose **Insert Table**.

In **Rows** and **Columns**, choose the number of rows and columns you want for the table.

Click **OK**.

Task 2: Putting Text in Table Cells

Click

Tab⇥
or
Click

A table without content is like a house without furniture. Here's how to start filling in your new table by putting text in **cells**—the boxes formed by the walls of each row and column.

✓ **Formatting Table Text**
You can apply to text in a table any of the character formatting from Part 3, including fonts, sizes, bold, italic, underlining, or a special color. Making the text in all cells of the top row bold, italic, or a unique color is a nice way to create column headings that stand out.

✓ **Aligning Table Text**
If you apply alignment (refer to Part 3) to text in a cell, the text is aligned relative to the cell it's in, not the page. For example, if you apply center alignment to text in a cell, the text is centered within that cell only. Other cells are not affected.

1 Click in the cell in which you want to type.

2 Type whatever you want.

3 Press the **Tab** key to jump to the next cell (or click in the cell you want to fill next).

Task 3: Putting Pictures in a Table

Most tables are mostly text. But you are not limited to only using text in tables. You can give your table added panache by using pictures.

Adding Links to a Table

You can also put links in a table. Just add to the table the text or picture you want to use as the link source, highlight that text or picture in its table cell, and create the link as usual (refer to Part 4). Actually, a table makes a lot of sense for a list of links; it lets you organize them and even add comments or graphics, such as ratings or new site flags.

Click

Click

 Prepare the GIF or JPEG image you want to insert (refer to Part 5), and store it in the same folder as the Web page file that contains the table.

 Click in the cell in which you want to put a picture.

 Click the **Insert Image** button on the Standard toolbar.

(4) **Click**

(5)

(6) **Click**

(7) **Click & Drag**

(4) In **From File**, type the filename of the picture file.

(5) Click **OK**.

(6) Continue adding pictures to cells until you've added all the pictures for this table.

(7) On each picture, drag a sizing handle (refer to Part 5) to scale the picture to the size you desire. The row and column sizes automatically change to fit.

✓ **Formatting Pictures in a Table**
You can use any of the picture formatting techniques from Part 5 on a picture in a table cell. To open the Image Properties dialog box to format a picture in a cell, point to the picture, right-click, and choose **Image Properties** from the pop-up menu.

End Task

Task 4: Adding a Caption to a Table

Start Here

If needed, you can add a *caption* (a descriptive title directly above or below the cells) to clarify or give instruction.

Click

Click

✓ **Adding Captions to a Table**

FrontPage Express automatically puts captions above the table, but you can move a caption below the table, too. Click anywhere on the caption, click **Table**, and then choose **Caption Properties.** A dialog box appears, giving you two choices for caption placement: **Top of Table** and **Bottom of Table.** Choose the one you want and click **OK**.

1 Click anywhere in the table.

2 Click **Table** and choose **Insert Caption**.

3 Type your caption. It appears above the table.

End Task

Task 5: Dressing Up Tables with Borders

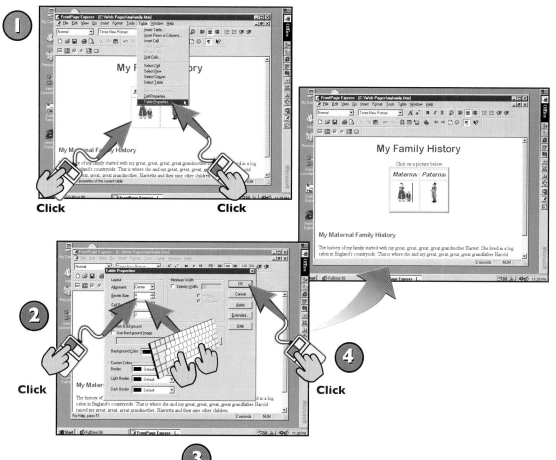

Click   **Click**

Click   **Click**

So far, you've learned how to use a table to line up content in rows and columns. But you might feel something is lacking—possibly lines to delineate the content and make the table look sharp.

① Click anywhere in the table, click **Table**, and then choose **Table Properties**.

② Click the box next to **Border Size**.

③ Type a number for the width of the borders. For example, type **4** to create a border 4 pixels wide. The higher the number, the thicker the border.

④ Click **OK**.

✓ **Adjusting Cell Spacing**
On the Table Properties dialog box, the box below Border Size—Cell Padding—allows you to adjust the spacing between the contents of a cell and the walls around the cell. Raising the number in Cell Padding, to, say, 3 or 4, creates more space around the cell contents, making the cell seem less crowded.

Task 6: Choosing Custom Border Colors

A table border is not one line, but three lines, used together to create a 3D effect. These lines are: a basic border line, a light border (a highlight on the top of horizontal lines and on the left side of vertical lines), and a dark border (a shadow on the bottom of horizontal lines and on the right side of vertical lines). You can choose the color for each part of the border.

✓ Trying On Different Looks

To experiment with borders, border colors, and anything else on the Table Properties dialog box, make any changes on the dialog box, then click the **Apply** button instead of **OK**. The changes are made in the table, but the Table Properties dialog box remains open, so you can try different settings without having to reopen it. Keep experimenting, clicking **Apply** each time, and then click **OK** when you see the combination you want to keep.

Start Here

Click   Click

Click

① Click anywhere in the table, click **Table**, and then choose **Table Properties**.

② In the Custom Colors section, choose a color from each of the three lists: **Border**, **Light Border**, and **Dark Border**.

End Task

Task 7: Choosing a Background for a Table

Unless you add a background to a table, the page's background color or image shows through the table (but does not obscure the table's content or borders). But a table can have its own background, different from that of the page, to make the table—and more importantly, its contents—really stand out.

✓ **Alternating Background Schemes in a Table**
You can use a different background for selected cells; for example, to make column headings stand out. In step 1, click in a cell, click **Table**, and then choose **Select Cell**, **Select Row**, or **Select Column**.

✓ **Background Images Override Color**
If you choose both a background image and a background color, the background image overrides the background color. However, you want to choose a background color that is close to the color of your background image, so your table text will show up even before the image loads.

① Click anywhere in the table, click **Table**, and then choose **Table Properties**.

② To add a solid color background, open the list next to **Background Color** and choose a color.

③ To add a picture background instead of a background color, click the check box next to **Use Background Image**. Then type the name of the GIF image, or **Browse** for it.

④ Click **OK**.

End Task

Task 8: Creating an Interactive Form

A *form* is a page that collects information from your visitors by prompting them to select options from lists, check check boxes, enter text, and more. While this *Easy* book can't effectively show you how to create forms from scratch, it can show you how to use the Form Page Wizard to create your own form.

✅ **Inserting Fields on the Fly**

You can use the buttons on the Forms toolbar to insert *form fields*—list boxes, check boxes, and so on—in any Web page. Just click in the page where you want the form field, click the button, and answer any questions FrontPage Express asks.

✅ **Choosing the Right Form Tool**

For a beginner, using the Form Page Wizard makes more sense than using the Forms toolbar. The wizard helps organize and encode your form correctly.

Click

Click

Click

Click

Click

1 From FrontPage Express, click **File** and choose **New**.

2 Click **Form Page Wizard**, then click **OK**.

3 Click **Next**.

4 In the **Page URL** and **Page Title** boxes, type a filename and title, and click **Next**.

Click

Click

Click

Click

Click

Click

Click

Click

Click

Click

5️⃣ Click **Add** and then click **Next**.

6️⃣ Click **Contact Information** and then click **Next**.

7️⃣ Check to select or clear the check boxes for the types of contact information you want the form to collect and then click **Next**.

8️⃣ To add additional questions, click **Add** and type your question in the text box, or to accept the default question, click **Next**.

Creating an Interactive Form Continued

Form Page Wizard

PRESENTATION OPTIONS

How should the list of questions be presented?

- as normal paragraphs
- as a numbered list
- as a bulleted list
- as a definition list

Click ⑨

Would you like a Table of Contents for this page?

- yes
- no

The wizard can align form fields using HTML tables or formatted paragraphs. Some older web browsers may not support tables.

☑ use tables to align form fields

Click ⑩

Cancel   < Back   Next >   Finish

Form Page Wizard

OUTPUT OPTIONS ⑫

How do you want to handle the input generated by users when they submit a form?

- save results to a web page
- save results to a text file
- use custom CGI script

enter the base name of the results file:

formrslt

name: formrslt.htm

Click

< Back   Next >   Finish

Click

Form Page Wizard

PRESENTATION OPTIONS

How should the list of questions be presented?

- as normal paragraphs
- as a numbered list
- as a bulleted list
- as a definition list

Would you like a Table of Contents for this page?

- yes
- no

The wizard can align form fields using HTML tables or formatted paragraphs. Some older web browsers may not support tables.

☑ use tables to align form fields ⑪

Cancel   < Back   Next >   Finish

Click

Click

⑨ Choose how you want the list of questions displayed on the Web page by selecting the appropriate choices.

⑩ Choose whether or not you would like a table of contents (unless you have a long list of questions, you most likely will not need this option).

⑪ Select whether or not to use tables to align your form fields. It doesn't hurt to use this option—it makes your form fields more presentable) and click **Next**.

⑫ Choose how you want the form to submit the form information, enter the form name (or accept the default name), and click **Next**.

Next Step

Click

Click **Finish**.

Make any additional changes to your form and be sure to save it.

✅ **Changing Your Form's Appearance**
You can edit the new page any way you like, such as formatting, adding text or pictures, and more. Just be careful not to delete the form fields.

✅ **Exploring Different Form Types**
This task demonstrated only one of the many different types of forms you can create by making different choices in the Form Page Wizard. Feel free to experiment.

Publishing Your Page Online

A play is not just lines on a page. Even after it is written and published, it does not officially become a play until an audience sees it on stage.

The same philosophy applies to a Web site. Even though you have created it, a Web site does not become real until it is published on the Internet. In this part, you find places on the Internet you can copy or upload your pages to the Web and more.

Tasks

Task 1: Finding Space on a Web Server

To be seen through the Web, your pages must be stored on a Web server. So, your first step is finding some Web server space to put your pages. It's likely you can get some space free from the *Internet service provider* (ISP, the company you pay for Internet access) or online server (such as America Online) you use. But, if you can't get free space there, you have other options to explore, which are described here in decreasing order of desirability.

✓ **Determining Needed Server Space**
How much server space do you need? Well, a single Web page file with text and a few pictures is usually smaller than 100 kilobytes (about 1/10th of a megabyte). So even a Web site made up of 10 or 12 different pages might fit in less than a megabyte of server space, unless your site includes a plethora of pictures or large media files, such as video clips.

 Start Here!

 Call the Internet service provider (ISP) or the online service you use (or check out your service's Web page), and ask whether you can use some space on that company's Web server.

② If the company you work for or the school you attend has its own Web site, they might let you use some space, particularly if your page is work or school related.

③ Go to Yahoo! (**www.yahoo.com**) or your favorite Web search tool, and enter **free Web space** as a search term. The search results will include companies offering free space.

 Next Step

4 GeoCities is a company that offers free server space in exchange for the right to put advertising on your pages. Check out **www.geocities.com**.

5 Talk City is a fairly new service offering the same basic deal as GeoCities, but a different selection of tools for doing it. Explore **www.talkcity.com**.

✅ **Adhering to Host Requirements**

GeoCities and Talk City both require special steps for putting your page online. These requirements include insisting that you join the GeoCities or Talk City community first, that you include their ads on your pages, and that you follow some unusual procedures for publishing your page (different from those you learn in this book). If you want to use one of these services, explore their Web sites thoroughly to learn the rules for joining and publishing.

After you choose your server, you need to know some stuff about it before you can publish there. Your ISP might give you this info over the phone, but ISPs can be hard to talk to. It is sometimes better to get this information online, if it's available there.

✅ **Rounding Up the Needed Info**

The information you need for publishing includes: The URL of the server (for example, www.myserver.com), the name of the directory in which you will store your files (usually the same as your username on the service), a password for copying your files to the server (often the same one you use to connect to the Internet), and the address of the server to which you will copy files (it might be the same as the final URL, but it might be a different address beginning with the letters ftp).

Task 2: Learning More About the Server You've Chosen

Click

Click

1. Go to the Web home page of the ISP, online service, or other organization from which you will get server space.

2. Look for links to User Homepages, Uploading Files, or other links that appear to lead to information about publishing your pages.

3. When you locate the information, click **File**, and then choose **Print** to print the information so you can refer to it while publishing your pages.

Task 3: Getting Ready to Publish

Drag

Drop

Publishing is usually pretty easy. However, problems have been known to occur. Most publishing problems happen not because publishing is difficult, but because the author failed to put his or her ducks in a row before starting the publishing steps. Here's how to get those ducks lined up smartly.

1 Check that all the files making up your page or pages—HTML files, images, and any other files your page delivers through links—are all stored in the same folder.

2 Delete or move from the folder anything that is not a part of the Web site, including any stray files or other folders.

3 Open your page and give it a final once-over, checking style, spelling, and links to bookmarks and files.

Most server providers prefer that you upload—copy your Web files from your PC to the Web server—using an Internet tool called *FTP*. If you're familiar with FTP, you can do it that way. But Microsoft's Web Publishing Wizard—which is installed automatically when FrontPage Express is installed—can automatically publish via FTP, and in a few other ways, too. So if you don't already know FTP, there's no need to learn now—at least for publishing purposes.

Closing Your Web Browser to Publish

If your Internet setup permits you to connect to the Internet without opening your Web browser, or to close your Web browser without disconnecting from the Internet, do that when you connect for this task. You don't need your Web browser while publishing your files, just your Internet connection.

Task 4: Running the Web Publishing Wizard

Click►

Click

Click

Close FrontPage Express and any other programs you might have open, and connect to the Internet.

Click **Start**, click **Programs**, choose **Internet Explorer**, and choose **Web Publishing Wizard**.

Click **Next**.

Click

Click

Click

④ Type the complete path to the folder where you store your Web page files, or click **Browse Folders** to select it from a dialog box.

⑤ If a check mark appears in the **Include Subfolders** box, click to deselect it.

⑥ Click **Next**.

⑦ Type the server name and click **Next**.

✓ **Updating Your Site**
If you want to publish a single file (such as an HTML file you've updated since you last published, see Task 5), add the filename to the end of the path in step 5. Only the file will be published—not all files in the folder.

Click

Click

Providing a Web Address

The URL you type in step 9 is the URL your visitors will use to visit your pages on the Web. To access your index.html file, they need only enter the URL exactly as shown in step 9. To access a Web file (other than index.html), they enter the URL, a slash (/), and then the filename; for example, www.ij.net/gcarrillo/ harriets.html.

8 In the upper box, type the complete **URL** of the server and directory in which your page will be published, and then click **Next**.

9 Type the URL of your Web site and click **Next**.

Next Step

Click

Click

Click

Click

Choose your dialup method, select your network or dialup, and click **Next**.

Click **Finish**. Wait while the Wizard uploads your pages to the server and then click **OK**.

✓ Determining Your Publishing Password
If you get server space from your ISP, your username and password will probably be the same ones you always use to connect to the Internet.

If you find that you need to fix or update something on a page that you have already published, it is not a problem. You can't edit the copies of your pages stored on the Web server; instead, you simply make changes to the original files on your PC, and publish only those pages you changed. The changed files automatically replace the old ones on the server.

Task 5: Updating and Editing Your Page

Click

Click

Click

✓ **Republishing Is Easy**
Republishing is easier than publishing the first time, because the Web Publishing Wizard remembers all the entries you made the first time for the server address, the folder containing the Web page files, and so on.

1 Edit or expand your pages in FrontPage, however you want, and check your pages carefully after changing them. Do steps 1, 2, and 3 of Task 4.

2 Click **Browse Files**, locate and select the file you changed, and click **Next**.

3 Complete the remainder of the wizard, just as you did in Task 4, and on the final dialog box, click **Finish**.

Task 6: Viewing Your Page Through the Internet

After you publish, you must test your Web pages through the Web, viewing it exactly as your visitors will. Besides, it's fun to see it online.

1 Open your Web browser and connect to the Internet.

2 In the **Address** box, type the Web page URL for your new page (including the filename of the HTML file you want to view), and press **Enter**.

3 Explore your page, evaluating its appearance and testing all your links. If you find any mistakes or anything else you want to change, refer to Task 5.

✓ Opening the Default Page

If you named your top page **index.html** (as suggested in Part 2), that page opens automatically when a visitor surfs to the server directory without specifying a filename. For example, if the user enters the URL **www.server.com/harriet/** in his browser, the index.html file in the harriet directory opens automatically.

Task 7: Getting Multiple Browser Programs for Testing

So your page looks great in FrontPage Express and in your own Web browser. But that does not necessarily mean it will look great to everyone. There are subtle differences between browsers and those differences can make a page that looks great in one browser not look so great in another.

✓ Seeking Help

To download programs from the Internet and install them, see Part 10.

✓ Ensuring Browser Compatibility

If your page looks good in FrontPage Express, you can rest assured it will probably look fine in either Netscape Navigator or Internet Explorer, which means it will look fine to the majority of folks online. Still, there are small, subtle differences between even the most recent versions of these programs, so it's still smart to test in both and adjust your files as necessary.

Click   **Click**

① You can find browser programs lots of places online, but a good place to start is **tucows.mcp.com**.

② Click the button for your system: **Win 95/98** or **Win NT**.

③ In the Browsers and Accessories box, click **Browsers**.

④ Scroll through the list, and use the links provided to learn about and download a variety of browsers you don't already have.

⑤

Install each browser you want to test with according to its instructions, connect to the Internet, and view your Web pages in the new browser.

⑥

Use the browser to surf to your page and evaluate the page's appearance.

⑦

If you see major flaws that would make the page impossible to read, adjust the page in FrontPage Express, retest it in the new browser offline, and then republish it.

✅ **Testing Pages Offline**

If you can figure out how to open *local files* (Web pages stored on your hard disk) in a particular browser, which can sometimes tricky, you can test pages offline by opening the Web files from your hard disk in your browser.

✅ **Changing Your Default Browser**

When you install some browsers, they might try to make themselves your *default browser*—the one that opens automatically when you open a Web page file (refer to Part 2). If an unwanted browser makes itself the default, you can usually restore your original browser to its "default" status by reinstalling it.

Task 8: Getting Your Own Domain

If you simply take some space on someone else's server, your page will be accessible through the Web, but it won't have the sort of catchy Web address that gives you a Web identity, such as `www.buick.com`. Instead, your page's address is expressed as a directory on the server; for example, `www.servername.com/harriet/`. If you want to have your own Internet name—and have the cash—a domain is the way to go.

✅ **Mastering Your Domain**

When typing your proposed domain in step 3, don't precede it with the "http://" or the "www" part, nor the ".com" at the end of the proposed address. These parts of the address are typical Web address parts, but not really part of the domain. For example, if you want your Web site address to be `http://www.wild.com`, just type `wild` in step 3.

Click

Think about what you want your Internet domain to be—for example, `www.harriet.com`.

Visit the Network Solutions Web site—the official organization that registers Internet domains, at `www.networksolutions.com`.

In the **Search** box at the top of the page, type the domain you chose in step 1, and click **Go**.

Paying for Your Own Domain Name

Most ISPs will register a domain for around $50. In addition to the setup fee, the ISP will collect an additional $70 from you to pay a required registration fee to **Network Solutions**. That pays for your domain for two years; after that, you must pay **Network Solutions $35 per year** to keep the domain.

 Choosing the Domain Type

The final part of the domain name can be **.com** (commercial site, the most common), **.org** (nonprofit organization, such as a foundation), **.edu** (educational institution), or **.net** (network). You'll be given a choice of which ones are available.

 Registering a Domain Yourself

You can register your domain yourself, if you know how, (saving the ISP's setup fee, but not the $70 due to **Network Solutions**) by filling in the forms provided on **Network Solutions'** Web site.

 If Network Solutions displays a report that your proposed address is available, proceed to step 5. If your proposed address is already taken, return to step 1 and try a different name.

 You can ask your ISP to register a domain for you or find another service by searching for `domain registration service`.

PART 8

Announcing Your Page

After you have published your site to the Web, you need to get the word out on the street that you are open for business.

Of course, the scale of your Web site promotion efforts should match the ambitions of your page. If your page is just a personal home page for family, friends, and the occasional passing stranger, using just a couple of these methods—such as announcing by email—will suffice. Most people who publish Web sites do so because they **want** to be found by as many Web visitors as might have an interest in the site. This part shows you ways that help you get noticed.

Tasks

Task 1: Finding Places to Promote Your Site

Before beginning to promote your site, you should do a little surfing to locate the pages where you might want your page featured. Certainly the list includes the major search engines such as Yahoo!, Excite, and AltaVista, but it also includes smaller directory pages that feature links to pages covering the same topic as your site.

Start Here

Click

Click

✓ Adding Your Site to a Search Engine

Most of the search engines have their own programs, called *crawlers* or *spiders*, that automatically search the Web and add new sites, using each site's title and contents to automatically determine which subject categories to list it in. But a few require you to manually add your site; you learn how to do this in Task 2.

1 Visit each of the major search tools, and look for links to information about adding or suggesting a new site.

2 You can gain one-stop shopping to all the major search pages by going to **www.searchthe.net**.

3 Click the **Visit Site** option button, and then click the search engine button you want to visit.

Next Step

(4) For any topic your page is related to, do a search to find pages covering that topic.

(5) Some of those pages will include directories of links to related sites.

(6) Send email to the Webmaster of sites containing directories, asking to have your site added to the list.

Ensuring Your Page Gets Listed
The search tools with crawlers will find your page within a few weeks after you publish it. But the pages containing subject-specific directories rarely have crawlers; if you want to get listed there, you need to contact the Webmaster.

Yahoo! is the most popular directory on the Web. It's also one that does not catalog the Web automatically—you must add your site to Yahoo! to ensure that searchers find your site when doing a Yahoo! search on a term that's related to your site's contents.

Task 2: Listing Your Page in the Yahoo! Directory

✓ **Choosing a Yahoo! Category**
If the category you choose in step 2 is too broad, Yahoo! will display a message to that effect, and ask you to choose another, more specific category before proceeding.

In your Web browser, go to Yahoo! at **www.yahoo.com**.

Use Yahoo!'s search box, or browse through its category listings, to go to a category in which your site belongs.

Scroll to the bottom of the page on which your selected category list appears, and click **Suggest a Site**.

Read the Suggest a Site page for tips on properly listing your page with Yahoo!.

Next Step

Click

Click

5 Scroll to the bottom of the Suggest a Site page, and click **Proceed to Step One**.

6 Scroll down to the Site Information form, and type the title and URL of your page or site, plus a brief description.

7 At the bottom of the Suggest a Site page, click **Proceed to Step Two**.

8 Continue through steps 2, 3, and 4, filling in all information requested and clicking the button at the bottom of the page to proceed to each new step.

✓ Describing Your Page to Yahoo! Users

The description you type in step 6 will appear in the search results whenever someone's Yahoo! search finds your page. Word it carefully, to help searchers determine whether your page contains what they want. Be sure, also, to include in the description keywords that are related to the page's topic.

End Task

Task 3: Listing Your Page in the Excite Directory

Start Here

Listing your page on Excite is much simpler than doing so in Yahoo! Excite uses a program to search through each site's pages, using the page's contents to determine which categories to list it in. So all you have to do is let Excite know where your site is—the program does the rest.

Click

Click

✓ **Waiting for Your Site to Appear**
After you manually add your site to Yahoo! or Excite, it probably won't show up right away. Typically, it takes about two weeks for your site to show up in the listings.

(1) In your Web browser, go to Excite at **www.excite.com**.

(2) Scroll to the bottom of the page, and click **Add URL**.

(3) Fill in the **Your URL** of your page (or top page of your site) and **Your Email** address, so Excite can contact you if necessary.

(4) Click **Send**.

End Task

Task 4: Checking Out the Site Submission Services

Start
Here

Click

You can promote your site effectively by simply adding it to Yahoo! and the directories on a few related pages, and then waiting for the crawlers to get you listed in most other search tools. Also, there are commercial site submission services. They submit your site to all the major search tools, plus hundreds of other directories. The fee for the service ranges from under $10 to more than $100.

 In the box at the top of the main Yahoo! page (www.yahoo.com), type site submission and click **Search**.

 In the search results, read the descriptions to find sites that offer site submission.

3 Visit the sites to learn what the service offers (and what it costs).

✓ **Submitting Your Site with Software**
There are also site-submission software packages you install on your PC. Check out a product called Submissions at www.submissions.com.

Task 5: Adding Your Web Address to Ads, Letterhead, and More

Some of the best places to publicize your page are not online, but off. All those big companies put their Web site addresses on billboards, in newspaper ads, and in TV commercials for a reason. You can advertise your site in your own way too.

Making Your Address More Visible

Wherever you can do so without disrupting the design of your printed publications, print the URL in a bright, unique color to make it stand out—just the way it does online.

Brevity Is the Soul of Web Addresses

These days, it's not necessary to include the prefix "http://" when showing your URL in print. That's great, because leaving off the prefix makes the URL look shorter, less technical, and easier to remember.

1. Add your Web site address to your stationery, business cards, business or personal newsletter, and advertising.

2. For a business or personal site, put out a special flier announcing your Web site.

End Task

Task 6: Announcing Your Page by Email

Click

Of course, the best source of visitors for your Web page is the pool of people already online. You can reach them most effectively using email. An email announcement to friends, clients, or customers is a great way to inaugurate a new Web site.

✅ Sending Links Via Email
After you type the URL, most email programs automatically create a link out of the URL you typed. This way the recipients of your email can just click the link and go straight to your site.

✅ Adding Pizzazz to Your Email
Email is letterhead, too. People with their own Web sites add a note at the bottom of all their email correspondence—an *email signature*—listing their Web site address. Outlook Express and other email clients let you create such a signature; consult your program's Help file or documentation to learn how to do so.

① In Outlook Express (Internet Explorer 4's email program) or other any other email program, type an announcement message.

② Address the message to recipients. Use a distribution list or type each email address in the **To:** line, separating each with semicolons (**;**).

③ Enter a meaningful and enticing **Subject** line.

④ Type your message and don't forget to include your URL. Click **Send** to transmit it.

End Task

PART 9

Super Editing: HTML

OK, so you have created HTML files by writing the HTML code yourself. And, that's what FrontPage Express created, behind the scenes, each time you created a page. HTML is the code that all Web authoring programs create.

The HTML file itself is just an ordinary tag language that uses the filename extension .htm or .html to identify and distinguish it from other languages. Inside the file, you find the text of your page and its title, plus an array of little codes, called *tags*. The tags are what makes HTML work. When a browser opens an HTML file, it reads and obeys the tags, which tell the browser what each object is (a heading, a paragraph, a link), the filenames and positions of any pictures, the URLs the links point to, and so on.

Actually, Web authoring programs are so easy to use that you could perceivably continue to progress as a Web author and never actually touch raw HTML. However, even with an *Easy* introduction to Web authoring, it's a good idea to at least explore the basics of HTML.

Tasks

Task 1: What Is HTML, Exactly?

A good way to begin understanding HTML is to explore the HTML file of your own Web page. That way, you can often guess what many of the tags are doing, because you created it yourself, which will give you a good idea of how the HTML tags do their thing.

Click

✅ Color My World

In its HTML view, FrontPage Express color-codes the HTML tags to help authors see them. But the color-coding doesn't really mean anything, and when you create your own HTML tags, you certainly don't have to worry what color they are!

1. In FrontPage Express, open a simple page you've created.

2. Click **View**, and then choose **HTML** to see the raw HTML code of the page.

Next Step

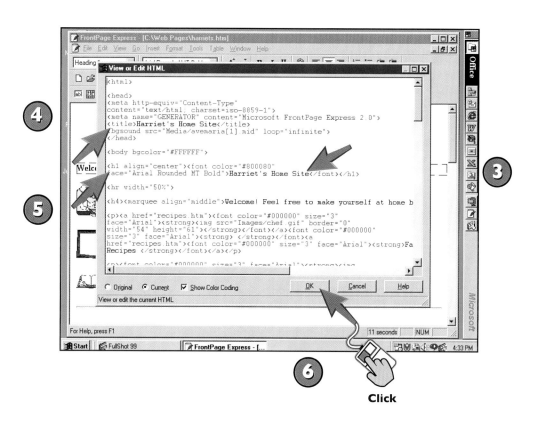

Click

Pairing Up

If you look closely at the tags, you'll notice that most (but not all) work in pairs. For example, somewhere near the top of the file, you'll see the tag <title>, followed by your page's title, followed by another tag, </title>. That's how tags usually work; one tag marks the start of something, and another tag (the same, only with the added slash at the front) marks the end.

3 Examine the page, ignoring the tags and looking for content you put there: your words, the filenames of pictures, the URLs of your links.

4 Now look at all the HTML tags, which are enclosed in carats (**< >**).

5 Observe that you can tell on sight what some tags do. For example, before text to which you've applied a level-1 Heading paragraph style, you'll see the tag <h1>—Heading 1.

6 Click **OK** to return to the regular FrontPage Express view.

End Task

Most of the job of creating a Web page in HTML involves typing tags and content. But first you need to understand the big picture, the way an HTML file must be organized into two sections: the header (which contains the page title, and sometimes other, optional stuff), and the body (the part of the file where you define everything you see in the page layout). Because an HTML file is just a text file, you can create it in any text editor, such as Windows's Notepad accessory.

✓ Capitalizing on Tag Style

When you type HTML tags, it doesn't matter whether you use uppercase letters (<H1>) or lowercase letters (<h1>). Some Web authors prefer using capital letters, because doing so makes it easier to see the tags buried within the text of the page. However, you can use either case.

Task 2: Creating a Web Page in HTML

Click

1. Click **Start**, then **Programs**, then **Accessories**, and then **Notepad**.

2. Type **<html>**, to mark the start of the file, and press **Enter** to start a new line.

3. Type **<head>** to start the header, and then press **Enter**.

Next Step

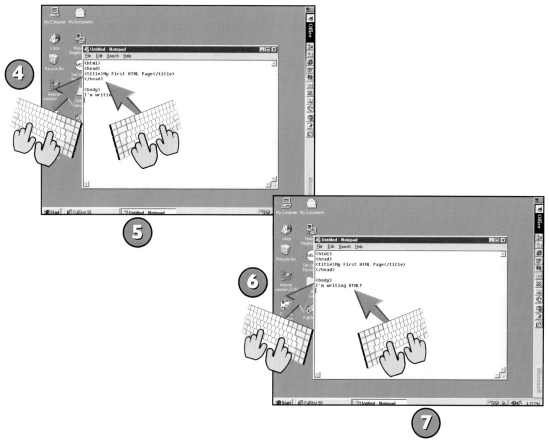

Using HTML in Addition to FrontPage Express

FrontPage Express does a lot for you, but it does not give you toolbar buttons or menu items for absolutely everything that can be done in HTML. That's why working in HTML is important. You can still save time by working primarily in FrontPage Express or another WYSIWYG (what you see is what you get) editor, then edit the HTML code directly to add tags your WYSIWYG editor does not supply.

④ Type **<title>**, type a title for your page, close your tab by typing **</title>**, and press **Enter**.

⑤ Type **</head>** to mark the end of the header and press **Enter**.

⑥ Type **<body>** to mark the start of the body of text and press **Enter**.

⑦ Type **I'm writing HTML!** and press **Enter**.

Creating a Web Page in HTML Continued

Click

Click

(✓) **Catching the Code**

Most browsers let you view the raw HTML code, called *source code*, of pages you're viewing. This enables you to learn about HTML by studying the pages you visit online. While viewing a page in Internet Explorer 5, choose **View** and then **Source**. In Navigator, choose **View** and then **Page Source**.

8 Type **</body>** to mark the end of the body.

9 Type **</html>** to mark the end of the file.

10 Click **File**, and then choose **Save**.

11 Choose a folder (or the desktop) to store the file in, type **practice.html** for the filename, and then click the **Save** button.

Next Step

Click

Double-Click

12 Click **File**, and then choose **Exit**.

13 In Windows, open the folder where you stored **practice.html**.

14 Double-click the icon to display the file in your default browser.

✅ Error-Checking Your Code

If you don't see what you should when you view the HTML file through a browser, it's usually because of a minor HTML coding error. If you forget to create both a header and body, or forget to use close tags (the ones with the slash in them, such as </body>), or misspell a tag, the browser cannot render or display the file correctly. If this happens, go back and check your tags carefully.

✅ Viewing Code with Notepad

When you choose **File, Open** in Notepad to reopen an **HTML** file you're working on, you won't see the **HTML** file in Notepad's Open dialog box, even after you navigate to the right folder. At first, that box shows only files ending in **.txt**. Open the list at the bottom of the Open dialog box, and choose **All Files (*.*)**. Then your **HTML** file will appear in the box so you can select and open it.

Task 3: Adding a Picture Through HTML

After you have the header and body set up in your HTML file, you can begin adding tags and content. To get a taste of how tags work, add a picture to your basic HTML file. Just for practice, use FrontPage Express's built-in HTML source editor to add the tag.

Click

Click

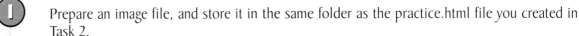

Click

Click

✓ **Seeing the Result of Your Changes**
To play with HTML, you can open this HTML view, make changes to the HTML codes or anything else on the page, and then click **OK** to return to FrontPage Express and see the results of your changes in FrontPage Express's regular "browser" view of the file.

Prepare an image file, and store it in the same folder as the practice.html file you created in Task 2.

Open FrontPage Express.

Click **File**, and then choose **Open**.

Click **Browse**, navigate to the folder (or desktop) where practice.html is stored, click **practice.html**, and click **Open**.

Click

Click

5 Click **View**, and then choose **HTML**.

6 In the body, between your line of text and the closing body tag, type **<IMG SRC=** (the start of the HTML tag that inserts an image in a page).

7 Follow the equals sign (=) with a quote mark ("), the filename of the image file, another quote mark ("), and a close carat (>).

8 Click **OK** to close the HTML editor and view the page in FrontPage Express.

✅ **Seeing Changes FrontPage Express Makes**
When you create a file in Notepad or another text editor, then view its source through FrontPage Express, you'll notice tags you never wrote, and other minor changes. FrontPage automatically adds some optional tags and deletes unnecessary (but harmless) line breaks in the HTML coding.

✅ **Undoing HTML Coding**
If, when you view the page back in FrontPage Express view, you don't like the results of the last HTML change you made, you can undo it by clicking **Edit**, and then choosing **Undo**.

End Task

Page
143

The tag that adds images is a little unusual, in that it doesn't work in pairs like most tags. To get a better sense of how tags usually work, add tags to apply level-1 heading format, center the heading on the page, and make a word within the heading *italic*.

✓ Aligning Your Alignment Codes

Observe the fact that the *align* tag goes *inside* the **<h1>** tag. Some special tags, called *attributes*, go inside other tags to modify the for-matting applied by the main tag. The align attributes (center, left, right) go inside the tags for a paragraph (**<p>**), heading (**<h1>**, **<h2>**...), and image (**<img src**...) to align those objects.

✓ Starting New Paragraphs

To add more paragraphs to your sample file, simply pressing **Enter** to start a new line doesn't work. You must start each new paragraph with one of the heading tags (**<h1>**) or with a new paragraph tag (**<p>**).

Task 4: Applying Formatting to Text

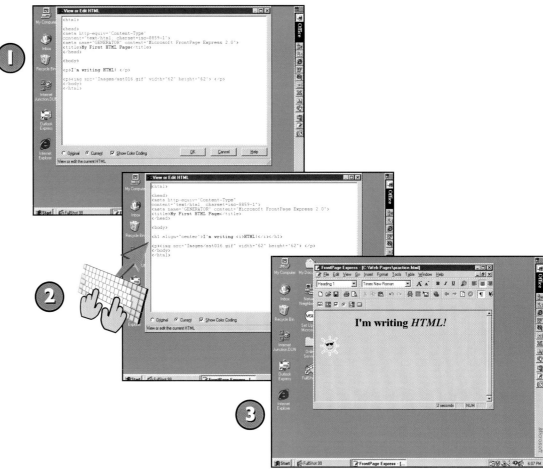

1. In FrontPage Express or Notepad, open the practice HTML file you created in Task 2.

2. Add the tags as shown previously to apply header 1 formatting (**<h1>**, **</h1>**), center the paragraph (**align="center"**...) and add italic (**<i>**, **</i>**).

3. View the page in your browser or in FrontPage's regular view, to see the results.

Task 5: Learning How to Use All the HTML Tags

Click

If you want to learn more about **HTML**, there are several good ways to get started. Not surprisingly, many of the best beginner's **HTML** primers and reference guides can be found online. *The 24-Hour HTML Café* is a good place to start.

 Be Aware of Version Changes

HTML changes from time to time, which is why you see choices for information about **HTML 3.2** and others for **HTML 4.0**. The older version usually contains 99% of the same tags as the newer version, and is more stable. So beginners are better off studying the older standard first, when a choice is offered.

Reading Further

Dozens of books can tell you how to use all the **HTML** tags properly. The creator of the **HTML Cafe**, **Dick Oliver**, wrote *Teach Yourself HTML in 24 Hours*, which is a good choice for an author newly graduated from *Easy Web Page Publishing*.

① Connect to the Internet, and go to the Macmillan Computer Publishing resources page for Web Publishing, at **www.mcp.com/resources/webdesign/**.

② Scroll down to the link for **24-Hour HTML Café** and click the link to **HTML 3.2**.

③ The 24-Hour HTML Café page opens.

PART 10

Discovering Other Web Authoring Tools and Techniques

With nothing more than FrontPage Express and the occasional bit of HTML editing, you can do most of what other Web authors do.

Before you leave this *Easy* book, it's important to know that there are other tools and utilities you can add to your Web authoring arsenal—especially now that you've developed a solid foundation through the tools you've learned.

In particular, there are other general-purpose Web authoring programs that can serve special needs or when you're ready to move up to more advanced tools. You'll learn a few such programs in this final part. I will also show you how to find other programs and resources online that will expand your Web-publishing prowess.

Tasks

Task 1: Finding Authoring Programs on the Web

There are many Web-authoring tools, including commercial, shareware, and freeware programs. New tools appear all the time. So being aware of the best-known tools (as you will be, after the next few tasks) isn't enough. To keep up with what's new and where to get it, you need to know how to search for the Web authoring tools available online. Here are a few ways to start.

Start Here

Click

✔ Trying Other Search Terms
Other good search terms to try in step 2 include **HTML editor**, **HTML authoring**, and **Web publishing**.

✔ Giving Other Products a Trial Run
When searching, pay particular attention to lesser-known, little tools, especially shareware products. Often these are more innovative than the popular tools you hear about the most.

1 Go to the Yahoo! search page at **www.yahoo.com**.

2 In the **Search** box, type **Web page authoring**, and then click **Search**.

3 The search results will show many categories and sites you can browse to find authoring programs and other Web authoring stuff.

Next Step

(4)

(5)

Click

(6)

Click

(4) You can also find plenty of tools by visiting the TUCOWS library at `tucows.mcp.com`.

(5) Click the button for your system: **Windows 95/98** or **Windows NT**.

(6) Look in the **HTML Tools** box for likely links, such as **Editors Beginner**, and click.

✔ **Adding Special Effects**
In the **HTML Tools** box on **TUCOWS**, notice the link for **Special FX**. This link leads to fun tools for adding animation, sound, and other pizzazz to your pages.

✔ **Seeing What's New**
Note the links in **TUCOWS's** far-left column. The **What's New** link offers a quick way to check for the latest tools.

✔ **Looking for Links**
If you want to try other search sites on your own, check out **CNET's** `builder.com`—it has some great links to explore, too.

End
Task

Task 2: Learning About Microsoft FrontPage

On the one hand, Microsoft's FrontPage, big brother to FrontPage Express, is the logical next step up for someone who's already experienced with the junior Express version. Although FrontPage offers you many powerful capabilities not included in Express, nearly everything you know how to do now is done the same way in FrontPage. So, it's an easy and logical step up. On the other hand, FrontPage isn't free. While trying to decide on your next move, visit the FrontPage Web site to learn more.

✓ Trying FrontPage for Free

Note that, at the writing of this book, Microsoft was offering a free 45-day trial of FrontPage using a link on the FrontPage Web site for a small fee ($6.95). When you visit, keep your eyes out for such offers, so you can try before you buy.

1 Connect to the Internet, and point your browser to **www.microsoft.com/frontpage/**.

2 Explore the links to learn more about FrontPage and how to get it.

Task 3: Learning About Netscape Composer

Just as **FrontPage Express comes free with Internet Explorer 5, Composer, Netscape's Web authoring program, comes free with Communicator, Netscape's all-in-one Internet software package. Composer is very similar to FrontPage Express, but it does a few things Express doesn't. For example, it gives you better control of the positioning of pictures on a page. Those capabilities make Composer a nice companion to FrontPage Express.**

✓ Getting More Detail on Netscape Composer

The book *Teach Yourself to Create a Web Page in 24 Hours* is not only a good next book for someone who started with *Easy Web Pages*, but also one that shows in detail how to use **Composer.** The book includes **Communicator** (with **Composer**, of course) and other **Web-authoring** tools on its free **CD-ROM.**

① Point your browser to **home.netscape.com/browsers/**.

② Explore the links to learn more about Communicator and Composer.

Task 4: Finding Graphics Utilities and Other Helpful Programs

So far, you've already discovered several good online sources for programs, including **TUCOWS** (tucows.mcp.com). But **TUCOWS** alone doesn't offer the incredible range of programs and files available from Download.com—your first stop when you want to find and download graphics utilities and other useful Web-authoring accessories.

✅ **Finding Graphics Utilities and Web Authoring Tools**
Download.com and similar sites (such as Shareware.com) are great for finding smaller, accessory-type tools—such as graphics utilities—but not for big tools, such as your primary Web authoring program. For those, it's better to go to the home page for that tool (or use Yahoo! or another search tool to locate the home page) to get more detailed information about the program than Download.com supplies.

Click

Click

Click

1. Go to Download.com at **www.download.com**.

2. Click the **Multimedia and Design** category.

3. Click **Image Editing**.

4. Scroll through the list of Image Editing programs and files, and click one that looks interesting.

5

Click

5 Read the description, and if you want the program, click the **Download Now** link.

✓ **Installing the Software**
If you're not experienced with downloading and installing programs from the Web, see Task 5 for instructions.

End Task

Task 5: Downloading Programs from the Web

If you've downloaded and installed programs from the Web before, you don't need this task. But because this book has shown a variety of great places to download programs, clip art, and more, it's only fair to cover the basics of downloading.

✓ Accessing Compressed Files

Often, the files and programs you download from the Web are *zipped*, compressed into an archive file so that they take up less space (and thus download faster). A zipped file uses the filename extension **.zip**, and its icon looks like a clamp around a file cabinet. Before you can use the contents of a zipped file, you might have to decompress it—*unzip* it—with a program such as WinZip (see Task 6). Other zipped files are *self-extracting*; that is, you just double-click the file's icon and the files decompress by themselves.

Start Here

Click

Click   Click

Click

Click

Click

Click

1. Go online, navigate to the link for downloading the file, and click it to start the download.

2. Choose **Save This Program to Disk**, and then click **OK**.

3. Use the **Save In** list to choose the folder in which to save the downloaded file. But don't change the filename. Then click **Save**.

4. The download begins. When the download is finished, a message appears to tell you so. Click **Close**.

 End Task

Task 6: Downloading WinZip

Click

Click

Double-Click

A shareware program, WinZip is just one of several programs available online for unzipping zipped files. You know you have downloaded a zipped file when the file's extension is .zip and its icon looks like a file cabinet caught in a clamp. After you have WinZip, you'll be equipped to handle the larger Windows programs and files available online.

✓ Using WinZip to Extract Files

After WinZip is installed, you can unzip files by double-clicking the file's icon, which opens the file in WinZip. In WinZip, you click the **Extract** button to unzip the open file.

✓ Creating Archives with WinZip

WinZip not only unzips, but also zips. You can use WinZip to zip up multiple files into a single archive file, which saves space wherever you store the file. Archiving is a great way to preserve your Web pages as they evolve.

---

① Go to www.winzip.com.

② Click the link labeled **Download Evaluation Version**.

③ Scroll down and click the link for the **Windows 95, 98 and NT** versions to begin the download.

④ After the download is complete, double-click the **WinZip** icon to install WinZip.

Task 7: Learning About Advanced Authoring Techniques

So, what's on the horizon now? As a budding Web author, you're ready to begin exploring some not-so-*Easy* authoring techniques, such as Java and JavaScript (used for programming scripts that expand a Web page's capabilities beyond plain HTML), advanced multimedia, and more. For help, here are some good places to begin your next Web adventures. Another good site is Microsoft's MSDN Web Workshop at `msdn.microsoft.com`.

Start Here

(✓) **Starting Your Study**
Probably the best place to start exploring Developer's Edge is by clicking the **Documentation** link in the left column, which leads to a variety of manuals for Web authoring techniques.

1 For an extensive selection of tutorials, reference pages, and other advanced authoring resources, visit Netscape's Developer's Edge site at `developer.netscape.com`.

2 For a more modest and simple selection of authoring tips, go to the InformIT page at `www.informit.com/webedit`.

3

Click

✅ **Learning from the Pros**

For many *Easy* readers, much of the material on Netscape's Developer's Edge site might seem too technical. Still, the site is so thorough, it's an excellent place to get acquainted with the vocabulary of advanced Web authoring—even if the result of that experience is simply the decision that your Web authoring ambitions do not exceed FrontPage Express!

✅ **Checking Out More Useful Info**

Observe the links along the left side of the InformIt Web page. These links lead to all sorts of valuable information.

3 To find specific information, you can perform a search or select a topic from the **Select Topic** drop-down menu.

End Task

alignment The way text is placed on a page. Left-aligned text lines up to the left margin, right-aligned text lines up to the right margin, and centered text is centered between the left and right margins.

animated GIF A special kind of GIF (Graphics Interchange Format) image file that plays as a brief, animated clip when viewed through a browser.

background A color or image that covers the entire area behind the text and pictures of a Web page.

bookmark An invisible marker on a Web page that provides a spot to which a link can point, used to take a visitor straight to that specific spot on the page. Bookmarks are also known as *targets* or *anchors* in some Web authoring programs.

browse To wander around the World Wide Web portion of the Internet, viewing Web pages through a browser. This is also known as *surfing* or *cruising* the Net.

browser A program, such as Internet Explorer or Netscape Navigator, that enables you to view Web pages.

bulleted list A list of items in which each item is preceded by a marker, a "bullet" or some other symbol character. *See also* numbered list.

CGI Short for *Common Gateway Interface*. One method for creating interactive sites, such as those that use scripts to make advanced Web page features work, such as forms. *See also* Java, JavaScript.

character formatting Formatting that changes the style of characters, such as applying fonts, bold, or italic.

check box A small, square box used to select objects in a program or a Web page. Clicking an empty check box inserts a check mark there, indicating that the object or option next to the check box is selected.

close tag An HTML tag required at the end of a block of code. For every beginning tag, there must be close tag. Close tags begin with **</**, for example, </bold>.

dialog box A box that pops up in Windows programs to provide the options necessary for completing a particular task. Different tasks display different dialog boxes.

domain The address of a computer on the Internet. A user's Internet address is made up of a username and a domain name. Every Web server has its own unique domain and can play host to other domains, as well.

download The act of copying information from a server computer to your computer. *See also* upload.

email address The Internet address an email program uses to send email to a specific Internet user. The address is typically made up of a username, an @ sign, and a domain name (**user@domain**).

FAQ file Short for *Frequently Asked Questions file*. A computer file, often made available on the Internet, containing the answers to frequently asked questions about a particular topic or Web site.

font A particular style of text.

form A part of a Web page in which users can type entries or make selections that are then collected and processed.

freeware Software available to anyone, free of charge (unlike shareware, which requires payment), often available for download from the Internet.

FrontPage Express A Web page authoring program from Microsoft, included in the free Internet Explorer suite of Internet programs (for Windows 95 and NT) and also built into Windows 98.

FTP Short for *File Transfer Protocol*. The basic method for copying a file from one computer to another through the Internet, often used for publishing Web page files by uploading them to a server.

GIF Short for *Graphics Interchange Format*. A form of a bitmapped file format (image file), commonly used for inline images in Web pages.

heading A short line of text, often set large and bold, that marks the start of a specific section of a document, such as a Web page.

horizontal line In a Web page, a straight line that divides sections of the page horizontally. Sometimes known as a *horizontal rule*.

HTML Short for *Hypertext Markup Language*. The document formatting language used to create Web pages. The files produced by Web authoring programs like FrontPage Express are HTML files.

hyperlink *See* link.

inline image An image that appears within the layout of a Web page.

Internet A large, loosely organized internetwork connecting universities, research institutions, governments, businesses, and other organizations so that they can exchange messages and share information.

Internet Explorer A browser created by Microsoft, which is used to view Web pages. Internet Explorer version 5 is built into Windows 98, and is available free for other systems (Windows 95 and NT, Macintosh, and UNIX). Most versions of Internet Explorer 5 include FrontPage Express.

intranet An internal, corporate network, usually a local area network, that is based on Internet technologies. It is used just like the World Wide Web—through a browser.

Java, JavaScript Two different methods for creating scripts, used for some advanced Web page features, such as interactive forms. *See also* CGI.

JPEG Short for *Joint Photographic Experts Group*. A form of an image file, usually photographic pictures, commonly used for inline images in Web pages.

link Short for *hyperlink*, an object on a Web page that takes the visitor to another page, downloads a file, or starts some other action.

link source The part of a link that a visitor actually sees on a Web page and clicks to activate the link. (The other part of a link is the URL.) A link source can be text or a picture.

list box In a dialog box or Web page, a small box with a downward-pointing arrow on the right. Clicking the arrow opens a list of options the user can click to select.

mailto link A link in a Web page that, when clicked by a visitor, opens the visitor's email program and creates a new message, preaddressed to a particular person.

marquee A line of text that repeatedly scrolls across part of a Web page, used as an attention-getting device.

menu A list of choices on a computer screen. A user selects one choice to perform an action with a software program.

Mosaic A browser, available as freeware.

Navigator Sometimes called Netscape, a popular browser from Netscape Communications. Navigator is available in a suite, called Netscape Communicator, which also includes programs for Web authoring, email, and other tools.

netiquette   The code of proper conduct (etiquette) on the Internet or the Net.

Netscape   Short for **Netscape Communications**, a software company that developed and markets Navigator. Some people casually refer to Navigator and Communicator as "Netscape."

network   A set of computers interconnected so that they can communicate and share information. Connected networks together form an internetwork.

Notepad   A program included with all versions of Windows which allows the user to view, edit, and print plain text files, such as HTML files.

numbered list   A list of items in which each item is preceded by a number, and the numbers go up as the list goes down. **See also** bulleted list.

paragraph formatting   Text formatting, such as paragraph styles or alignment, that can be applied only to a whole paragraph or paragraphs, never to only selected characters within a paragraph, like character formatting.

paragraph style   The principal form of text formatting on a Web page. Paragraph styles include six levels of headings, a style for normal text, and several different styles for creating lists.

search engine   A program that provides a way to search for specific information on the World Wide Web, such as Yahoo!.

selection   Text or a pictures that the author has highlighted so that the next action the author performs affects only the highlighted text or picture(s).

server   A computer on a network, used to store information and "serve" it to other computers that contact it through the network. A Web server stores Web pages, which it serves to the browsers that tap it through the Internet.

shareware   Software programs that users are permitted to acquire and evaluate for free. Shareware is different from freeware in that, if a person likes the shareware program and plans to use it on a regular basis, he or she is expected to send a fee to the programmer.

signature   A block of text on a Web page, usually near the bottom, that identifies the page's author or the Web master. Signatures often include a mailto link to the author's email address.

surfing   Another term for **browsing** the Internet.

symbol   A character that's not on the keyboard, such as a copyright symbol. In FrontPage Express, you add symbols to your pages from a special dialog box.

table   A box or grid used to arrange text or pictures in neat rows and columns.

tag   A code in the HTML language.

title   The name that identifies a particular Web page. A Web page's title appears in the title bar at the very top of the browser window.

toolbar   In a program, a row of icons or buttons, usually near the top of the program's window, you can click to perform common tasks.

undo   A feature of FrontPage Express and some other programs that enables you to reverse an action you performed, if you change your mind. You can reverse several actions.

upload   The act of copying information to a server computer from your computer. **See also** download.

URL   Short for **Uniform Resource Locator**. A method of standardizing the addresses of different types of Internet resources so that they can all be accessed easily from within a Web browser.

Web   **See** World Wide Web.

Web site   A group of individual Web pages linked together into a single, multi-page document. A Web site is sometimes used to describe a whole Web server, or all pages on a particular domain.

Webmaster   The person responsible for the management and maintenance of a particular Web page or Web site. This person is sometimes (but not always) the Web page author.

WinZIP   A Windows program used to compress files into archives so that they can be uploaded or downloaded more quickly and conveniently. Also used to decompress files later to restore them to their original state.

wizard   Automated routines, used throughout Windows, for conveniently performing a step-by-step procedure, such as setting up Windows or configuring it for the Internet.

World Wide Web   (WWW or Web) A set of Internet computers and services that provides an easy-to-use system for finding information and moving among resources.

Yahoo!   A popular search engine.

A

B

C

captions, tables, 100
carats (< >), HTML tags, 137
case sensitivity, HTML tags, 138
CD-ROMs
   clip art, 75
   Internet Explorer, ordering, 5
cells (tables)
   spacing, 101
   text, adding, 97
Center button, 42
character formatting, 32, 45
clip art, 74-75
Clip Art Connection Web site, 90
Close command (File menu), 24
closing Web pages, 24
color schemes, 70-71
colors
   background, 70-71
   custom, 71
   table borders, 102
   text, 48-49, 70-71
   transparent backgrounds, 78
columns (tables), 96
commands
   Edit menu
      Bookmark, 60
      Redo Clear, 37
      Undo Clear, 37
   File menu
      Close, 24
      Page Properties, 26
      Save, 23

Format menu, Bullets and
   Numbering, 44
Insert menu
   Horizontal Line, 72
   Marquee, 86
   Symbol, 35
Table menu
   Insert Caption, 100
   Insert Table, 96
   Table Properties, 101
Tools menu, Follow Hyperlink, 66
View menu, HTML, 136
Composer, 151
contact information (Web pages),
19
Copy button, 38
copying
   pictures, 75
   text, 38
   URLs, 53
Create Hyperlink button, 56, 85
Create Hyperlink dialog box, 85
cursors, 34
custom colors, 71
Cut button, 39
cutting and pasting text, 39

D

Decrease Indent button, 41
Decrease Text Size button, 46
default browser, 121
default colors, 71
Define Custom Colors button, 48
deleted text, recovering, 37
deleting text, 36
dialog boxes
   Create Hyperlink, 85
   Horizontal Line Properties, 73
   Image Properties, 82
   Marquee Properties, 87
   Page Properties
      Background tab, 70-71
      General tab, 92-93
   Saving, 6
   Table Properties
      background, 103
      border colors, 102
      borders, 101
digital pictures, 76
direction (marquees), 87
dividing pages, 72
domains, 122-123
Download.com Web site, 152
downloading
   files, links, 62-63
   FrontPage Express, 6-7
   Internet Explorer, 6-7
   programs, 154
   WinZip, 155

links

M

N - O

P - Q

R

S

Underline button